2nd EDITION Well-Managed SCHOOLS

Also from the Boys Town Press

Tools for Teaching Social Skills in School

More Tools for Teaching Social Skills in School

Positive Alternatives to Suspension

Building Resiliency in Youth: A Trauma-Informed Guide for
    Working with Youth in Schools

Building Resiliency in Children: A Trauma-Informed Activity Guide for Children

Building Resiliency in Teens: A Trauma-Informed Workbook for Teens

Everyone's Talking

Take Two: Skill-Building Skits You Have Time to Do!

13 & Counting: Be the Difference

13 & Counting: Does a Hamburger Really Have to Be Round?

13 & Counting: Rescue Me

GRIT & Bear It!

GRIT & Bear It! Activity Guide

Zest: Live It

Zest: Live It Activity Guide

Effective Study Strategies for Every Classroom

School Administrator's Resource Guide

Working with Aggressive Youth

Teaching Social Skills to Youth

Adolescence and Other Temporary Mental Disorders (DVD)

No Room for Bullies

No Room for Bullies: Lesson Plans for Grades 5-8

No Room for Bullies: Lesson Plans for Grades 9-12

Safe and Healthy Secondary Schools

Teaching Social Skills to Youth with Mental Health Disorders

Common Sense Parenting®

For a Boys Town Press catalog, call 1-800-282-6657
or visit our website at BoysTownPress.org.

Boys Town National Hotline®
1-800-448-3000
A crisis, resource, and referral number for kids and parents

STRATEGIES TO CREATE A PRODUCTIVE AND COOPERATIVE
SOCIAL CLIMATE IN YOUR LEARNING COMMUNITY

2nd EDITION Well-Managed SCHOOLS

Michele Hensley, M.S., Walter Powell, Susan Lamke, M.S.,
Scott Hartman, M.S., Michael Meeks, M.S., and Erin Green, M.S.

Boys Town, Nebraska

Well-Managed Schools, 2nd Edition

Published by the Boys Town Press
Father Flanagan's Boys' Home
Boys Town, NE 68010

Copyright © 2016, Father Flanagan's Boys' Home
ISBN 978-1-944882-02-0

Boys Town Press is the publishing division of Boys Town, a national organization serving children and families.

10 9 8 7 6 5 4

Table of Contents

School as Community

"I got into teaching so I could teach...."

> As an education major in college, Sharon remembers feverishly taking notes in Psychology of Adolescence, a core requirement of the program. She learned a lot of theories; so many, in fact, that she had two legal pads full of notes before the midterm. Talking about adolescent behavior in abstract terms seemed meaningful at the time. But when Sharon stood in front of her first classroom and actually had to lead students who cursed her and wouldn't follow basic instructions, she didn't need a theory to explain what was happening. She needed a strategy to deal with it.

"Very quickly I realized students demanded more from me than pure academic instruction. They needed emotional and behavioral support, too...."

According to the National Institute of Mental Health (2006, 2007), as many as 10 percent of children have mental health issues that are "severe enough to cause some level of impairment." One such disorder, Attention-Deficit Hyperactivity Disorder (ADHD), affects between three and five percent of all children.

The National Center for Children in Poverty (2006) estimates that nearly 24 million American children live below the poverty line. The percentage of adolescent children living in low-income families (both poor and near poor) has been on the rise, increasing from 35 percent in 2007 to nearly 41 percent in 2013 (Jiang, Ekono, & Skinner, 2016).

> The school where Terrence taught was in the heart of an economically depressed neighborhood. Street crime was so prevalent that getting to school safely was a legitimate concern for many. Terrence

wanted his students to know that education was their ticket to more and better opportunities. Getting them to continue to believe that message when they were outside his classroom was difficult. The neighborhood was rough, and the actions of students in the classrooms, hallways, bathrooms, and stairwells reflected the toughness that existed in their world. Many came from families that were struggling to survive. Some parents worked 80 hours a week just to make ends meet. Other parents were absent from their children's lives because of addictions, incarcerations, and simple indifference. Terrence had to be more than a teacher to some students; he had to be a father, brother, counselor, and friend.

"College prepared me well to teach a curriculum. Teaching others about life, not so much."

Life is about relationships. Classroom management is, too. This book is written to help you manage and enhance the personal and social dynamics that exist inside your classrooms and schools. The strategies and techniques described in the following pages specifically address issues of classroom management – issues that too often receive only a cursory mention in many of the academic programs that prepare and certify today's classroom professionals (DePaul, 1998).

Whether you're a teacher, administrator, support staff member, or school volunteer, you need a range of skills and a broad knowledge base to manage student behaviors and maintain orderly environments. Helping students feel emotionally and physically safe is as important as the academic instruction itself. After all, students who come to class late, won't stay seated, talk out of turn, bully, and start fights disrupt your teaching and distract you from your academic goals. These behaviors can also create an unsafe and unwelcoming environment. Students who act inappropriately and disrupt the learning process undermine the very reasons they are there – to be empowered with the knowledge and skills they need to reach their full potential and realize a simple truth that many may not believe: "I can be successful!"

These pages describe what we at Boys Town believe well-managed schools look and sound like, and what gets accomplished there. This image transcends any single individual or schoolroom to encompass the entire environment of one's learning community. Among the many elements needed to formulate our picture, special emphasis is placed on...

- Building relationships with all students.

- Encouraging a sense of connectedness to school for students.

- Establishing a safe, positive climate for learning.

- Empowering every child with the social skills needed to enjoy academic and personal success.

The words "well-managed" and "classroom" are not paradoxical. Rather, research and experience tell us that disciplined and supportive environments are not only possible, but also essential if students are going to have the best opportunity to learn. The difficulty, of course, is trying to develop and sustain a positive learning environment amid the many economic, social, cultural, and political forces that shroud today's educational landscape.

The Obstacles

An eclectic group of children and adolescents converge in America's classrooms and schools. They bring with them divergent histories, experiences, languages, and family lives. Their cognitive and social abilities vary, from the exceptional to the exceptionally challenged. From their diversity comes a broad range of opinions and attitudes about what is "acceptable" behavior, "appropriate" discipline, and "desired" outcomes. Differing perceptions and expectations about what happens, or should happen, at school mean that tension between and among teachers, administrators, parents, and students is virtually inescapable. This tension can have negative effects in the classroom.

In a 2004 survey on school discipline policies conducted by Public Agenda, a nonpartisan research organization, nearly 50 percent of teachers said they had been tagged with charges of unfairly disciplining students. More than 70 percent believed students who had chronic behavior problems should not be allowed in general education classrooms. Behavior issues and discipline problems prove so frustrating for some teachers that they quit the profession. In this survey, one in three teachers either thought about leaving or knew someone who had. And the National Commission on Teaching and America's Future (2003) found that about half of urban teachers quit within their first five years on the job. One commonly cited reason: poor student behavior.

Students, too, are frustrated. Many perceive their teachers as unfair and arbitrary when it comes to addressing behavior problems. In Public Agenda's 2006 Reality Check (a survey of minority families' perceptions of their schools), more than 30 percent of black students, more than one quarter of Hispanic students, and nearly 20 percent of white students agreed that their school is not consistent in its practices for enforcing rules on discipline and student behavior. Thirty percent of black students also thought very few of their teachers were respectful toward other students. Parents, too, can share this sense (valid or not) of disrespect and discrimination. The survey found that 40 percent of black parents, 31 percent of Hispanic parents, and 25 percent of white parents believed that in the last couple of years, a teacher had unfairly disciplined or punished their child.

Whether these beliefs are justified may be questionable. But less debatable is the fact that there are students and parents who feel their school has wronged them. Feelings of victimization and powerlessness – whether legitimate and understandable or not – negatively affect teaching and learning. In fact, when students perceive discipline as unjust and punitive, and sense a lack of respect and caring from teachers and staff, they can become disconnected from school. The more detached their feelings, the more at risk they are for engaging in problem behaviors that range from acting out in the classroom to drinking, smoking, and sexual activity (Libbey, 2004; McNeely & Falci, 2004; McNeely, Nonnemaker, & Blum, 2002; Catalano, Haggerty, Oesterle, Fleming, & Hawkins, 2004).

Students who feel alienated at school experience more episodes of emotional distress, violence, fighting, bullying, and absenteeism than students who enjoy caring relationships and feel a sense of belonging in their school environment (Resnick, Harris, & Blum, 1993; Blum, 2005). Sadly, according to Klem and Connell (2004), anywhere from 40 to 60 percent of high school students may be "chronically disengaged" from their school. This lack of attachment not only puts these students at risk for behavior problems, but also can negatively impact everyone else – parents, peers, and teachers – in the learning community. Valuable instructional time is sacrificed when disruptive and off-task behaviors dominate a classroom.

The sense some students have of being excluded or not fitting in at school is compounded if they also lack caring relationships at home. For some young people, school may be the only source of positive social support. Unfortunately, gang and street violence; domestic abuse inside the home; addictions; economic hardships; hunger; coercive, critical, or neglectful parenting; and other negative sociological and environmental stressors are the harsh realities for too many children. Young people exposed to these risk factors oftentimes develop disruptive and antisocial behavior patterns (Walker, 1998).

The behaviors and attitudes that students learn at home, on the street, and from an increasingly celebrity-obsessed, media-saturated culture are never left outside on the schoolhouse steps. They creep into our classrooms, cafeterias, and common areas. While some of these learned behaviors may be appropriate, others are aggressive, self-centered, and disrespectful. Regrettably, many youth – regardless of their social or economic status – have not acquired the social skills necessary to effectively and appropriately interact with peers and adults in school settings. When educators fail to provide any type of behavioral support or intervention, students' personal and academic success is threatened. For example, Olweus (1991) found that chronic school bullies who weren't properly disciplined for their bullying behaviors had a far greater risk of becoming incarcerated adults. Other researchers have found a relationship between social skills deficits and future delinquency (Bullis, Walker, & Stieber, 1998; Walker, Ramsey, & Gresham, 2004).

The issue of social skills or students' social abilities appears to be problematic for many educators. Some teachers – most notably those who work with adolescents and teens in secondary school settings – expect their students to already be socialized in appropriate school behavior. This attitude is born from the assumption that since young people have had years of schooling, formal social skills instruction is unnecessary. Other educators, regardless of grade level or position, view social skills as something that can be naturally acquired, without structured teaching. But Horner, Sugai, Lewis-Palmer, and Todd (2001) point out, "Expecting the students to arrive with a common, and consistent, set of social skills is naïve. Every student entering a school needs behavior support" (p. 78). They also note the futility in believing that "random social interactions" alone are enough to teach students the critical skills they need for success in the classroom. Youth who are never taught social skills will develop their own habits and devices for getting their needs met, habits and devices that often conflict with what most educators would consider acceptable behavior.

In our experience, when social skills instruction is not present in schools, neither are other meaningful proactive measures for shaping student behavior. Instead, rigid zero-tolerance policies, a reliance on traditional forms of reactionary punishment, and safety viewed strictly in terms of the number of resource officers or metal detectors in a building dominate. These strategies offer little in terms of developing a positive school climate or fostering trust among students and staff. In fact, such punishing or institutionalized environments may actually cause more behavior problems than they prevent (Olafson & Field, 2003; Astor, Benbenishty, & Meyer, 2004; Lewis, 1997; Noguera, 1995).

One explanation as to why social skills instruction and other intervention efforts aimed at student behavior may be getting shortchanged is the political climate. Both state and federal legislation are placing a premium on student achievement. Stakeholders – parents, community members, and government officials – are clamoring for greater accountability from their public schools. Testing has become a high-stakes game used to determine whether students are meeting their state's academic achievement standards. As the testing goes, so goes the money and the reputation. Sadly, when administrators and teachers have a singular focus on academic content and "teaching to the test," it's the emotional needs of students that are most at risk of being sacrificed (Kohn, 2004; Willert & Lenhardt, 2003).

The laundry list of potential obstacles – internal and external – one confronts when trying to build a supportive, healthy learning environment is long. Competing agendas and contradictions in schools and among stakeholders hamper efforts to create a sense of community. But all too frequently, the strategies employed to overcome these obstacles and improve student behavior only exacerbate the problems.

The Opportunities

You may be wondering why we have described certain obstacles that appear rooted in economic, social, and cultural factors that are beyond your sphere of influence. The fact is, the environmental realities of children's lives shape their attitudes, beliefs, and behaviors, and as a result, they impact you. Despite what may seem like challenges beyond your control, schools have a vital role to play in their communities. The Search Institute (2007), for example, identified 40 Developmental Assets that nurture young people and help them mature into caring, responsible adults. The more young people are exposed to or experience these assets (caring schools, supportive adult relationships, high expectations, and school engagement, to name just a few), the healthier their development and the better their outcomes. Your success in creating a safe and effective learning environment can help mitigate whatever negative influences confront students outside of school. Likewise, your success can build on and accentuate the positive assets that exist in the neighborhoods and communities where your students live.

But how does one go about building a sense of community, cooperation, and caring in school? How do you humanize the school experience for students so they feel valued, respected, and motivated? How do you manage student behavior so appropriate actions are rewarded and repeated and disruptive actions are discouraged and diminished? It won't be by happenstance. As Sugai, Sprague, Horner, and Walker (2000) note, "Schools that are safe, effective, and controlled are not accidents. They are environments where considerable effort has been made to build and maintain safe school cultures" (p. 94).

For educators who seek to overhaul or enhance the social climate of their learning community, the Boys Town Education Model® offers the structure and strategies needed to reduce disruptive behaviors and empower students with the self-management skills necessary to produce a well-managed, cooperative classroom.

The Boys Town Education Model

The Boys Town Education Model is a school-based intervention strategy that emphasizes behavior management practices, relationship-building techniques, and social skills instruction. The Education Model is rooted in applied behavior analysis and social learning theory. It evolved out of the Boys Town Teaching Model, which was developed more than three decades ago and is the bedrock of the philosophy of care used in our long-term and short-term residential programs for abused, abandoned, and at-risk youth.

In the following pages, you will learn components of the Education Model that can be universally applied in general education classrooms and common areas of your school. As an intervention strategy, it represents a comprehensive classroom management approach that emphasizes preventive practices rather than reactionary responses. In that regard, our Education Model is similar to, and reflective of, two other holistic models that are prominent in education literature and practices – positive behavior support and authoritative communities.

When a positive behavior support model is applied to school settings, the main objective is to fix or alter the environment so it becomes more nurturing and supportive of students' academic and social needs. As a result, problem behaviors become "irrelevant, inefficient, and ineffective" (Carr et al., 2002, p. 5). Typically, positive behavior support involves a three-tiered approach with primary, secondary, and tertiary intervention strategies. School-wide discipline practices and social skills instruction targeting all students in all settings (classrooms, hallways, gymnasiums, cafeterias, etc.) characterize primary intervention. These measures are universally applied to everyone, regardless of their academic and behavioral abilities (Sugai et al., 2000; Walker & Sprague, 1999). The strategies we advocate in these pages represent primary or universal interventions.

Research shows that universal interventions can be effective with as many as 80 percent of a school's student body (Colvin, Kame'enui, & Sugai, 1993; Taylor-Greene et al., 1997). In other words, those students adapt to the behavioral expectations and may not need more individualized, intensive secondary or tertiary interventions. This majority can serve as the anchor that maintains a healthy school climate, provided their positive behaviors continue to be encouraged and supported. The use of proactive measures, such as social skills instruction and well-defined and communicated behavioral expectations, help protect these students from adopting or developing disruptive behavior patterns (Sugai, Horner, & Gresham, 2002).

The benefits of social skills instruction, coupled with proactive classroom management practices (having rules, procedures, and consistent consequences), should not be underestimated. In a study of two schools that implemented our Well-Managed Schools program, office discipline referrals (ODR) decreased and ODRs for physically aggressive behavior decreased substantially. In addition, academic engagement increased and students' social skills, as indicated by the Walker-McConnell Scale, improved (Oats, Faulk, Gulley, Hensley, & Burke, 2006). The practices we advocate are an effective means of providing more positive behavior support to students.

The principles behind positive behavior support are also found in the idea of authoritative communities. This term, coined by the Commission on Children At Risk (2003), is given to social institutions or groups of people who are committed to one another and who model behaviors that demonstrate respect for self and each other. Individuals living and working in such life-affirming, values-oriented, and cooperative environments enjoy close relationships and strong bonds with one another. Sadly, the Commission found that America's social institutions, such as schools, families, and neighborhoods, are becoming increasingly disconnected. They are either inattentive or indifferent to the emotional, physical, and even spiritual needs of youth. This lack of caring contributes to broken and strained relationships, which the Commission cites as one explanation for the rising and unacceptably high rates of depression, mental illness, emotional distress, and behavior problems (aggression, school dropout, etc.) that afflict our youth. The Commission noted that adults are very responsive when it comes to treating these problems. There are effective pills and psychotherapies that have their place. But the root causes – the environmental factors – remain untouched by this type of treatment. And oftentimes it is the environment that has to change if children are truly going to thrive. Prevention has to be valued as much as treatment.

At Boys Town, we are well versed in the fundamentals of creating authoritative communities. Every day, we work to create such en-

IMPLEMENTING THE MODEL

Well-Managed Schools provides an overview of many, but not all, technical components of the Boys Town Education Model. This book is intended to be a useful resource or reference in your work to improve classroom management and the social climate of your school. Boys Town provides workshops, intensive skill-based training, and ongoing consultation services to educators and organizations interested in implementing all components of the Education Model. This book supplements those services. To learn more, call 1-800-545-5771 or visit www.boystowntraining.org.

vironments for the children and adolescents who enter our schools, hospitals, group homes, and shelters. As the Commission notes, "authoritative" doesn't mean manipulative control or coercion. Rather, it represents an environment with a shared vision, where youth have structure, clear limits, boundaries, and expectations, yet are also surrounded by caring, nurturing, and involved adults. These are the very principles that are embodied in our classroom management model. When implemented in education settings, the academic and social outcomes we all want for our students can be achieved.

Ultimately, "classroom management," "positive behavior support," and "authoritative communities" are theoretical concepts that are related to a single idea: Relationships. School is a social experience, but there are too many students, parents, and educators whose social interactions are strained, stressful, and unsatisfying. Instead of saying to students, "Get along," we need to teach them what "getting along with others" looks and sounds like. Instead of telling parents, "Stay away," we need to communicate about and encourage their participation. Too often the practices and structures of classrooms and schools give their stakeholders contradictory and confusing messages. The practices and strategies outlined in the following chapters are designed to break down barriers and overcome obstacles so you can create and sustain a productive, collaborative, and cooperative learning environment.

How to Use This Book

We have organized this manual into four sections, each of which contains chapters that relate to one overarching theme. The theme of Section I is "connecting with your students." Chapters on relationship building, problem solving, and the ABC's of behavior spotlight the value and importance of knowing your students. When you understand their motivations and limitations, you can more effectively respond to, change, or reinforce their behaviors. Section II examines how you can "increase opportunities for student success." Classroom practices, including establishing clear rules and procedures, are explained. We also introduce strategies for teaching students the social skills they need to meet the behavioral expectations you have in your classroom and school. Sections I and II emphasize the environmental factors that are conducive to shaping student behavior in positive directions.

In Section III, we explore the interpersonal dynamics of responding to student behavior. The value of recognizing the good things students do is emphasized along with how to effectively correct student misbehavior and handle emotionally intense situations without getting caught in a cycle of conflict. Finally, Section IV focuses on the role parents or primary caregivers can play in support of your efforts. The section concludes with a look at how to measure whether your efforts to improve student behavior and the overall social climate are producing the outcomes you want. Evaluation, which is sometimes referred to as Response to Intervention (RtI), is an ongoing process. Classrooms are dynamic environments. Any strategies and intervention efforts that work one semester or one year may have to be modified or replaced with other strategies to best support the changing social realities of your students.

We hope that when you get to the end of this book, you have a better understanding and appreciation of "school as community." The practices and strategies we advocate are designed to humanize the school experience. When students are motivated, when they feel good about the classroom environment and the relationship they have with you, when they can manage themselves and accept responsibility for their behavior, and when they feel empowered to improve, then the climate is more conducive for you to effectively teach and your students to truly learn.

Connecting
with Your
Students

IN THE 2004-2005 METLIFE SURVEY OF THE AMERICAN Teacher (2004, 2005), nearly 20 percent of new teachers said they were never given a tour of their school, including common areas such as libraries and cafeterias. Students had similar experiences. One in five was never told where to find his or her locker. Surprisingly, 25 percent of students didn't know where to go to get their lunch. In some cases, it may have been an accidental oversight or the fault of the teacher or student. Nevertheless, when staff and students are unsure of their surroundings, confusion and chaos can be common. And in our work with schools, we've seen environments where the prevailing attitude is more about "I" than "We."

The lack of a formal welcome is emblematic of a more disheartening problem. These statistics illustrate how some schools overlook or ignore the needs of their stakeholders, thus undermining any sense of community in the classroom or school. If students are going to feel more connected, you cannot leave them feeling lost – literally and figuratively. And it's difficult to see how you can address issues of emotional safety when the environment is impersonal and individuals are taken for granted.

RELATIONSHIPS MATTER

Dear Ms. Feser,
Just want to say, "Thanks." All those speeches you gave about never giving up and never settling for less meant a lot to me. You challenged me to do better, and pushed me to learn. I know I challenged you – usually not in a good way. Anyway, I appreciate the time you took to listen to me. Our little chats probably didn't mean much to you, but they always made me feel better. You made the difference in my life. Thank you.

— A GRATEFUL STUDENT

The content presented in the next five chapters examines ways in which you can strengthen the student-teacher bond. Chapter 1 outlines relationship-building strategies that include everything from simple acts of kindness to instructional techniques that make students feel more comfortable and confident. Chapter 2 looks at how to help students help themselves. You'll learn how to teach problem-solving methods so students of any age or developmental level can be empowered to make better choices. Chapter 3 explains how social learning theory supports our Well-Managed

Schools practices, and how you can apply the theory's principles to improve student behavior and interpersonal relationships. Chapters 4 and 5 highlight how your language can communicate fairness and objectivity to students, which is especially important when working with students who feel victimized and abused by the authority figures in their lives.

Building Relationships

America's youth are spending more time in school and on academic work than at any time in history. School-aged children between the ages of 6 and 17 spend nearly 33 hours a week at school, an average of 6 to 7 hours a day. As recently as the 1980s, the average was 5 to 6 hours a day in school (Juster, Ono, & Stafford, 2004). With more time being spent at school, the student-teacher relationship takes on even greater importance.

Your success at creating a well-managed school depends largely on the quality of the relationships you forge with students. Teacher-student relationships influence everything from the social climate of a school to the individual performance of a student. When students feel liked and respected by their teachers and peers, they enjoy more success in school – academically and behaviorally (Lewis, Schaps, & Watson, 1996; Baker, Terry, Bridger, & Winsor, 1997). Conversely, when interpersonal relationships are weak, communication is poor, and mutual trust and respect are lacking, fear and failure rather than safety and success characterize the social climate (Hernandez & Seem, 2004). And as Noguera (1995) notes, "When fear is at the center of student-teacher interactions, teaching becomes almost impossible" (p. 204).

Fortunately, a real sense of physical danger or psychological fear does not permeate most classrooms. Still, there are learning environments that use policies and procedures that promote apprehension and mistrust. The desire of some adults to establish and exert control over and demand compliance from students too often dwarfs efforts to create a sense of warmth, compassion, and fairness. As a result, many of the personal and psychological needs of students are never addressed. This is not to say that teachers knowingly or willfully ignore the non-academic needs of students. Rather, it reflects how outdated clichés such as, "Be tough," "Don't give an inch," or "Keep them busy and look like you're in charge" – once presented as simple prescriptions for effectively managing a classroom – continue to be ineffectively exercised in some schools.

The Value of Positive Relationships

The quality of students' social relationships influences how they perceive themselves as learners and unique individuals, how much responsibility they assume for their behavior, and how well they perform academically. Students cannot reach their full potential unless their teachers and others in the learning community encourage them through words and actions.

The nature and quality of the relationships you establish and maintain with students shows itself in the social climate of your classroom. The more supportive and positive the climate, the easier it is to have an instructional environment that is motivating and rewarding for students. By creating a classroom that is both open and trusting, you enable students to excel in many ways, such as demonstrating initiative, taking risks (asking more questions, volunteering answers aloud, etc.), and committing themselves to learning. The more you connect with students, the better able you are to promote growth and positive change in their behaviors. Also, the healthier your relationships are with students, the more likely they are to accept rules, procedures, and discipline decisions.

Of course, mutually rewarding and respectful relationships rarely develop in a matter of days, weeks, or even months. Nor can teacher-student relationships ever really be considered fully "developed." Instead, they continually evolve over time and across events and issues. Two key variables that significantly influence the way relationships grow are…

- The personal or affective qualities of the relationship.

- How you communicate or relate to your students.

Generally speaking, there is a common set of behaviors and attitudes that are both socially acceptable and generally valued by members of our society. These behaviors and attitudes include such concepts as honesty, sensitivity, concern and respect for others, a sense of humor, reliability, willingness to listen, and so on. Many students enter our schools and classrooms without these attributes because of poor role models or damaged learning histories, or simply because they did not have someone to guide them through a particular phase of development. As with so many other life skills, it falls on the school – and you – to teach students how they can develop positive adult and peer relationships (see Chapter 10). But in addition to teaching students essential social skills, you also need to maintain a high rate of positive interactions, engage in open, personal discussions, and show genuine interest in their activities beyond the subject matter you teach. All of these things help to humanize teacher-student relationships, as well as the school experience.

Quality relationships with students are especially important when you have young people who feel disconnected from school. Often, these students have a variety of behaviors that interfere with their social-emotional development and academic achievement. By improving the quality of your interactions with these students, you can help them engage in more appropriate behaviors and reduce the frequency and severity of their disruptive actions (Jones & Jones, 2007).

Strategies to Build Positive Relationships

Firmness. Compassion. A stimulating teaching style. According to students, teachers who possess these characteristics are more appealing and deserving of respect (Noguera, 1995; Woolfolk Hoy & Weinstein, 2006). And respect is the cornerstone of any healthy relationship. But what exactly does it mean to be firm or compassionate? And how do you communicate those values to students in a classroom?

We'll take a closer look at how to be firm in subsequent chapters on rules, procedures, and consequences. As for teaching style (or how you present content), it's important to note that students who are bored and disinterested tend to be more disruptive than students who are actively engaged in and excited by the instructional methods of the teacher. The purpose of this chapter, however, is about how you can bring compassion into the classroom and throughout the learning community.

Compassion can be defined as acts of kindness, expressions of empathy, signs of concern, displays of dignity, and demonstrations of respect. In the classroom or school, you can show your compassion by doing the following:

Be kind. There are many opportunities during a school day to show kindness to students. And kindness can take many forms. Smiling, for example, is a simple but powerful expression. A smile costs nothing but it is one of the richest gifts you can give to students. It can lift the spirits of those who may be feeling down while also showing them and others that you're friendly, approachable, and easy to talk to.

Welcoming students with letters or notes prior to the beginning of the school year or semester, or giving notes at other appropriate times, such as when a student has accomplished a particularly difficult task, shown significant behavioral improvement, or been elected to student council, are all friendly gestures that can strengthen relationships. The welcome mat, however, should always be out. Greeting students by name when they enter your classroom, walk through the hallways, dine in the cafeteria, or attend activities outside of school shows that you're happy to see them. It establishes the perception that you don't consider them a burden, a problem, or unworthy of your attention – which many may feel at home or among their peer groups. In addition, you're modeling good manners and demonstrating how "politeness" looks and sounds. When you're trying to create a welcoming environment, it makes sense to extend a hand or say "Hello," and teach students to do the same. Also, remembering to say "Thank you" when students volunteer, help out, or do anything that makes your job easier shows gratitude and respect.

Express empathy. Empathy can be used to show students how much you care about them and their success. This is crucial whenever you're addressing and correcting behavioral mistakes. Words that show understanding can defuse some of the anger or hurt children might feel. Empathy can be expressed vocally by using a soothing, caring tone. Expressions such as, "I know you're unhappy about what just happened," "I understand how disappointed you feel," or "I can see this is very important to you," are nonthreatening phrases you can use to start a dialogue with students who may be feeling angry, disappointed, or embarrassed. Teaching and modeling empathy can also have a positive effect on students' social relationships. This is especially true in environments where bullying is a problem.

Young people who bully or play the role of a bystander – one who does nothing to stop bullies or help victims – often lack empathy and perspective-taking skills. By helping students be more empathetic, you foster greater understanding and compassion, which are hallmarks of a positive school culture.

Show concern. Concern usually is shown when a student suffers a personal injury or experiences a traumatic life event. But showing concern doesn't have to be limited to these instances. You also can express concern by showing interest in students' activities and achievements beyond the classroom or subject you teach. When students excel in athletics, art, music, drama, or academics, congratulate them on their accomplishments. If a student earns an award for community service or for humanitarian work, recognize the effort. Ask questions about how the student got involved and what he or she hopes to do in the future. Informal chats on topics that are of interest to students are just one more way of reaching out and connecting with them.

You also can bond with students, as well as enjoy a good time with them, by participating in school activities such as "hat day," spirit week, post-prom parties, and other special events sponsored by the student council, various clubs, or other student or parent organizations. Your participation in such events communicates a commitment to their success and well-being that goes beyond the classroom.

Give dignity. In addition to these relationship-building techniques, Marzano (2003) recommends that teachers use the following strategies to build positive relationships by creating a cooperative classroom and being considerate of students who have differing learning styles and needs:

- When asking for answers in class, give students time to formulate their response instead of expecting instant replies or moving on before they have a chance to say anything.

- When students are unsure or confused, assist them by rephrasing your questions or clarifying what you want them to do.

- Show patience and listen. We expect students to listen to teachers and other adults in school, but how well do adults listen to the concerns, questions, and needs of students?

- When students offer input or ideas, acknowledge their suggestions and credit them rather than attributing it to yourself or no one.

- Encourage participation from all students by clearly communicating – verbally and behaviorally – the right of everyone to contribute to discussions and activities without fear of being ostracized or criticized.

- Increase positive reinforcement through supportive comments and gestures of affection (thumbs up, pats on the back, high-fives). At Boys Town, we believe that positive comments should outnumber negative feedback by at least four to one.

Communicate respect. The importance of using effective communication skills – making eye contact with students, answering questions pleasantly and enthusiastically, showing pleasant facial expressions, and using humor when appropriate – cannot be overemphasized. These components are what create warm and caring interpersonal interactions, which are critical if students are going to feel a sense of security, belonging, and respect in your learning community.

School Staff as Role Models

Research by noted psychologist Albert Bandura (1986) (*Modeling Theory/Social Cognitive Theory*) suggests that individuals tend to emulate the behaviors of significant others – individuals who are perceived as competent, trusting, and a major source of support, direction, and reinforcement. As a teacher, you embody these qualities. You're also in an excellent position, second only to that of the family, to serve as a role model for students.

At school, students learn by watching, just as they learn by doing. Observing the actions of others influences how they respond to their environment and cope with unfamiliar situations. As your students look at you, what messages does your behavior communicate?

Research suggests that the quality of your interactions not only affects the individual relationships you have with students, but also can influence students' perceptions of their peers. For example, one study found that peer-rejected students were less likely to experience continued rejection if their teachers liked them and communicated that through positive interactions. The opposite was true for peer-rejected students who were disliked by their teachers (Hughes, Cavell, & Willson, 2001; Taylor, 1989).

We witnessed such a phenomenon at an urban middle school. During a consultation, we sat in on a class to observe teacher-student interactions. In a span of five minutes, the teacher made the following comments to one student:

- "Rachel, pay attention."

- "Rachel, be quiet."

- "Rachel, you know your art supplies don't belong there. Put them where they belong – NOW."

- "Rachel, do you see how nicely Miguel cleaned up his work station? You need to do the same. Now, Rachel!"

Anytime something happened in this classroom, Rachel was singled out and admonished by her teacher – loudly and publicly. This happened even though other students were not paying attention,. and were being loud and misplacing their art supplies. The teacher's apparent dislike of Rachel reverberated outside the classroom. At recess, she was teased and badgered by classmates who mimicked the teacher's harsh tone. If the teacher could nag Rachel, then it must be okay for others to do the same.

This example, along with various research studies, illustrates how important it is for you and your colleagues at school to engage in interactions and behaviors that are compassionate and caring. Imagine if Rachel's teacher had offered an apology for singling Rachel out for discipline or had bothered to point out any of the positive things she did in the classroom. Rachel might feel better about herself, and her peers might not see her as a failure or as someone to be scorned.

Obviously, there will be times when disciplinary actions and verbal reprimands are necessary. There also may be times when the pressure of the job and your stress level causes you to be more harsh or critical than you normally would be. Those moments are going to happen. But they should not be the norm. All students, even the most challenging, need to receive positive comments and affirmations.

Final Thoughts

While we encourage educators to reach out to all their students, we want to caution against abandoning all professional boundaries for the sake of "connecting" with students. Trying to be a "friend" at the expense of being the authority figure is ultimately self-defeating.

Healthy teacher-student relationships share many characteristics of friendship – being kind, showing concern, spending time together, etc. – yet these relationships should not be viewed as true friendships. They're not. It can be tempting to relax or abandon personal or professional boundaries in an effort to bond with students. However, when boundaries are too lax or inconsistent, students can get confused about what's appropriate or mistakenly believe they can violate boundaries, too. This can lead to outrageously inappropriate conversations, acting out in provocative ways (sexually or aggressively), and other "boundary-free" behaviors that harm relationships and the learning environment.

We suggest teachers view their role in the classroom, and their relationship with students, as "in loco parentis" (in place of a parent). You are entrusted by parents to be responsible for their children's physical and emotional well-being. Therefore, your actions – including attire and appearance – should be guided by what is in the child's best interests.

As a teacher, you adopt and use specific verbal and nonverbal behaviors to elicit appropriate behavior from your students. The strategies you choose are going to be affected, positively or negatively, by the context in which they are used and the nature and quality of the relationship you have established with your students.

The quality of the teacher-student relationship plays a prominent role in how students will respond to the intervention strategies outlined in the coming chapters. Some of the strategies actually help strengthen the teacher-student bond while others depend more on an existing positive relationship to be most effective. Creating caring relationships with your students, however, will not resolve every

Reviewing Your Relationships

Use this checklist as a prompt to evaluate and reflect on the quality of the relationships you have with your students.

- ☐ Would my students describe me as a compassionate teacher?

- ☐ Do I communicate empathy, understanding, concern, and dignity to my students?

- ☐ How well do I know my students? Are there some who I know very little about? What can I do to strengthen my connection to them?

- ☐ Outside of school, do I know what my students like and dislike?

- ☐ Do I praise my students more often than I correct them?

- ☐ Am I too harsh when I correct them?

- ☐ Would my students describe me as genuine, insincere, or indifferent?

- ☐ Do I participate in school-related activities that are outside my normal teaching duties?

- ☐ What more can I do to reach out to students who struggle with behavior problems?

- ☐ Is my voice tone usually low and pleasant? Is my body language welcoming and relaxed or cold and tense?

- ☐ Do I see my students as interesting individuals, or do I dread seeing them?

classroom problem nor prevent issues from occurring. That's why concern and understanding must be delicately balanced with realistic limits, and clear and specific expectations.

2
CHAPTER

Problem Solving

Charlotte is in the seventh grade and often spends evenings online chatting with friends. In recent days she's received several messages from a classmate who says she has an eating disorder and sometimes cuts herself. Charlotte thinks the girl might be lying but wonders if she should tell a parent or guidance counselor.

After lunch, three high school buddies approach Peyton and ask him to ditch his afternoon classes and go with them to the beach. Peyton doesn't want to but he's afraid they'll think he's a wuss.

After school, a classmate asks Kelsey to write a book report for him and offers to pay for it. Kelsey would like to have the money but is afraid of getting caught.

During recess, two third-graders are chosen to be on the same soccer team; both want to be goalie and they begin arguing in front of the net.

Issues and problems like these are not unusual. Students face conflict, conundrums, confusion, and difficult choices every day. As a teacher, administrator, counselor, or support staff member, you invest as much time during the school day dealing with students' relationship issues and problem mediations as you do advancing their academic progress. Fortunately, many of the social interactions and events that occur at school can be monitored and used as real-life teaching and learning opportunities to help students develop problem-solving skills and support their social adjustment.

Problem solving is a life skill, one that students can use in or out of school, now or 15 years from now. There is no question that problem-solving skills are valuable to one's social adjustment. It has been said that psychological health is related to a problem-solving sequence that involves being able to recognize and admit a problem, reflect on solutions, make a decision, and take action. Furthermore, problem-solving ability might be among the factors that contribute to an individual's use of prosocial, rather than antisocial, behavior (Goldstein, 1999). Some research also suggests that improved problem-solving skills among students can lead to improved classroom behavior. Likewise, inadequate problem-solving skills generally result in a young person relying on socially inappropriate and ineffective solutions to real-life problems, particularly solutions that are aggressive or coercive in nature. Other research also indicates students who have behavior problems often struggle to identify choices when dealing with problems and are more likely to demonstrate rigid thought patterns.

Why do so many of our students lack the requisite skills needed to effectively solve problems? One of the most obvious reasons may be poor modeling. Experience and environment too often teach young people to resolve disputes and disagreements in ways that are more destructive than constructive. For example, if a student repeatedly watches his classmates withdraw or use avoidance to cope with bullying problems at school, he is likely to use those same tactics when bullied. While this may provide immediate relief, the problem remains, and the student is likely to be victimized again. If a student lives in an environment where adults settle disputes and obtain what they want by using their fists (shoving, punching, etc.) and their mouths (cursing, yelling, etc.), she learns to use those aggressive tactics to get what she wants on the playground or in the classroom.

Another contributing factor appears to be neurological in nature. In adolescence, the prefrontal cortex (the region of the brain thought to play an important role in one's ability to solve problems, plan, and make judgments) isn't fully developed. The emotional, sometimes irrational, choices young people make may be partly explained by the fact that their brains are still developing. Anthropologist Helen Fischer, quoted in Barbara Strauch's book, *The Primal Teen* (2003), says, "The prefrontal cortex develops slowly. They (adolescents) have strong drives but not the brain power or the experience to go with them" (p. 150). Neuroscientist Dr. Jay Giedd, also quoted in *The Primal Teen*, offers this noteworthy analysis of young people's prefrontal cortex: "They have the passion and strength but no brakes and they may not get good brakes until they are twenty-five" (p. 33).

As educators, we need to recognize that many of our students, including older teens, may not fully comprehend the consequences of their choices. Child psychiatrist Peter Jensen recommends that adults "talk through possibilities and options" with young people and take the role of "auxiliary problem-solver" so youth learn how to make more thoughtful, rather than impulsive, decisions (Strauch, 2003; p. 35).

Experience, environment, and biology all are contributing factors as to why many students respond inappropriately – retaliate, threaten, give in, lash out, etc. – to certain situations or are unaware that problems exist. All young people need help learning how to identify and solve problems.

What Is Problem Solving?

Problem solving is a behavioral process that offers a variety of potentially effective options for dealing with a problem, and increases the probability of selecting the most effective solutions from among the various options. Research suggests using a multi-step process for teaching youth problem-solving strategies that includes: 1) problem identification or general orientation; 2) problem definition; 3) generation of alternatives; 4) evaluation of the solutions; and 5) decision making (Spivack & Schure, 1974; Glasser, 1998).

Students who have a plan or strategy to follow when facing challenges in or out of school are more likely to succeed in recognizing and resolving problems. Problem solving can also be used retrospectively (with the luxury of hindsight) to help students make better decisions in the future. The Boys Town Education Model® uses the **SODAS** method, adapted from a counseling process developed by J.B. Roosa (1973), to teach students the general skill of problem solving.

SODAS is an acronym for the following steps:

S – Define the **SITUATION**

O – Examine the **OPTIONS** available to deal with the problem

D – Determine the **DISADVANTAGES** of each option

A – Determine the **ADVANTAGES** of each option

S – Decide on a **SOLUTION** and practice

This general framework for problem solving has a great deal of utility and flexibility. For example, you can use this process to conduct group problem solving, such as during a class meeting to discuss bullying problems or peer mediation sessions. Students can use the skill components to solve interpersonal conflicts, such as how to deal with peer pressure, or intrapersonal problems, such as what to do if homework is lost or textbooks are forgotten.

Regardless of whether the problem involves the entire class or an individual student, or is interpersonal or intrapersonal in nature, the primary focus of your teaching should be on using the process and teaching the students how to effectively use the SODAS method. When you introduce this process to students for the first time, be patient. It may take them a while for them to work through it. However, with practice, they will become faster and more proficient at working through all the steps.

Step 1: Define the Situation

The SODAS problem-solving process begins with you helping the student clearly define the situation or problem, assuming that the student is able to recognize that a problem exists. Not all students possess this skill and this may be where you need to start. A problem can be defined for students as a situation in which they need to do something to get what they want, but they don't know what to do or how to do it (Kaplan & Drainville, 1990).

Before a student can be expected to engage in the skill of problem recognition, he or she must first be able to recognize that a problem situation exists. To measure how well your students can recognize whether or not a problem exists, give them a pair of situations and ask them to decide if there is or is not a problem. Here is an example:

Situation #1:
"Candace gets home from school on Tuesday and realizes she left her science book in her locker. She has a unit test on Wednesday. Is this a problem? Why or why not?"

Situation #2:
"Shay gets home from school on Tuesday and realizes he left his science book at school. He has a unit test on Friday. Is this a problem? Why or why not?"

If you're helping elementary-age students recognize instances and non-instances of problems, more concrete examples and specific teaching, such as using pictures paired with a direct instructional approach, may be more appropriate. For example, you might show a second-grade class a picture of a child being bullied by older kids on a playground. You then could say something like this: "Here's a problem situation. Several older students are picking on you during recess. You want them to stop doing this but you don't know what to do to get them to stop. Why is this a problem?"

Once students can determine whether a problem exists, they are ready to define the situation or problem. This component of the skill is extremely important; many students who have difficulty problem solving know a problem exists but can't define it correctly. Oftentimes, students tend to leave themselves out of the problem, or their description of the problem is very vague and emotional:

- "I hate math class!"

- "Nobody in my class likes me."

- "My homeroom teacher isn't fair and she always picks on me!"

To pinpoint the specific problem, use general clarifying questions or statements to help the student more clearly focus on the issues. For example, you might ask, "Can you explain that further?" Or, you may need to ask more direct, specific questions to help the student talk about his or her issues, such as, "Why do you hate math class?" or "Why do you think your teacher is unfair and picks on you?"

As you explore the situation with a student, it's crucial that you engage in supportive verbal and nonverbal behaviors that communicate empathy, concern, and encouragement. Without these positive, relationship-building components, your questioning might sound more like an interrogation and cause the student to withdraw.

When a student more clearly defines a problem situation, summarize what he or she is saying. Summarizing is particularly important before any options are discussed. The summary can provide assurance that all relevant information has been reviewed and that you accurately understand the student's situation. If your summation is inaccurate or incomplete, the student then has an opportunity to correct any misconceptions. It's important to do this before moving on to identifying options. Without an accurate or clearly defined situation, it's nearly impossible to generate useful options or viable solutions.

Step 2: Examine the Options

The ability to generate a list of alternatives or options is probably the single most important problem-solving skill. The cognitive skill of knowing what to do in case of failure is one that can prevent or decrease a student's frustration level or the need to engage in impulsive behavior. Knowing how to pursue or select alternative options also may be all the encouragement a student needs to keep on trying and not give up (Kaplan & Drainville, 1990).

Once the situation is clearly defined, help the student generate options or potential solutions to the problem. Ask questions, such as, "Can you think of a way to handle that?" or "What do you think you can do about this?" It's important that students generate options that might actually solve the problem.

Initially, students may struggle to come up with options or think of more than one. Also, the suggestions they offer may not be very helpful or realistic. Whenever a student gives an option that sounds off the wall, try not to be judgmental. The purpose here is to help students learn to make decisions on their own. Rather than criticize or label an option as "good" or "bad," be objective by commenting positively about the student's participation in the process. A statement such as, "That's great! You've come up with a second option. You're really trying to think this through," offers encouragement and support. You can also remain neutral by prompting the student for more options by saying something like, "Okay. That's one option. Can you think of another?"

Avoiding judgmental statements can be very difficult, especially if the student suggests a solution that would only cause more problems, such as, "I'll just have to punch him out." You need to remember that your role at this point is just to get the student to generate options. Right now, you're just encouraging the student to brainstorm. In the next step, the student will examine the advantages and disadvantages of each option. That is when you can help the student judge the wisdom of his or her suggestions.

When students are identifying options, it's okay to offer your own suggestions. However, this should be done only after the student has given all of his or her ideas. When suggesting an option, it's best to phrase it in the form of a question, such as, "How about talking to your math teacher after class?" This way the student still feels involved in the process. Over time, students will feel more comfortable and be better able to generate options on their own. Once they can generate three or four different options for every situation or problem, they should be considered competent at this skill.

Steps 3 and 4: Determine the Disadvantages and Advantages

After students are able to generate several options for solving a problem, they need to learn how to evaluate or analyze the advantages and disadvantages of each. Evaluating the pros and cons of each option should be done based on the following criteria (Kaplan & Drainville, 1990):

- **Efficacy** – Will this solution help me achieve my goal without causing me (or others) any additional problems?

- **Feasibility** – Will I be able to take the action outlined in my options?

At this stage, your role is to act as a guide, helping the student think through the efficacy and feasibility of each option. In a sense, you are attempting to teach the student there is a cause-and-effect relationship between his or her decisions and what happens to him or her. If the student has trouble thinking through the advantages and disadvantages, you can help by asking more specific questions. You might say something like, "What do you think would happen if you cursed at your teacher or just stopped going to class?"

There may be a number of advantages and disadvantages for any given option. Again, since the goal is to help the student learn to think, it's important to solicit as many advantages and disadvantages as possible.

Remember, too, to remain nonjudgmental and avoid arguments with the student about his or her perceptions. We understand this can be difficult when a student seems enthusiastic about the un-realistic advantages of an option ("Yeah, it'd be great to fight it out because then he'd leave me alone and everybody else would think I'm a badass.") or fails to recognize the obvious drawbacks (being expelled, getting hurt, etc.). Rather than argue about an advantage, simply acknowledge or rephrase the student's viewpoint. You could say something like, "Okay, so you think that an advantage would be...." Later, you can guide the student's judgment when discussing the disadvantages by posing thought-provoking questions, such as, "What happens if you lose the fight?"; "Could you get hurt or hurt someone else?"; or "What will the principal do if he hears you were fighting with another student?"

If a student clearly does not see or cannot verbalize an important advantage or disadvantage, you should offer your viewpoint and al-low the student to react.

After discussing the disadvantages and advantages for all the op-tions, do a summary review of each one. This will reinforce the cause-and-effect relationships for students.

Step 5: Decide on a Solution, then Practice

The last step in the SODAS process involves having a student choose a solution from one of the options he or she has identified. After examining the advantages and disadvantages of each option – with your guidance – the student most likely will select a workable solution. It may not always be the best course of action from your point of view, but if the student's choice isn't going to hurt anyone, is not illegal, and does not contradict the values of your classroom or school, let it stand. It's important that the student feels he or she "owns" the solution. You want the student to feel comfortable imple-menting the solution and committed to making it work.

After the student selects an option, encourage and reassure him or her that the solution can be successfully executed. You can offer support by telling the student you're willing to answer any questions he or she has about how to implement the solution successfully. You can also enhance the chances for success by role-playing or practic-ing with the student on how to carry out the option.

The role-play scenarios should be as realistic as possible. Often, you will know the people the student needs to interact with when implementing a solution (friends, classmates, employers, principals, other teachers, coaches). Because you know these individuals, you can simulate their behaviors. For example, if a student's coach is fairly abrupt and somewhat stern, it's best to portray the coach in a similar manner. To make the role-play as realistic as possible, demonstrate several different reactions or responses the student might encounter. The more prepared the student is to handle differing reactions, the more likely it is that he or she will be successful.

While it's important to show confidence in the student's ability to implement the solution, you shouldn't promise him or her that the option will **BE** successful. There are too many variables the student can't control. Instead, ask the student to check back with you after he or she tries to implement the solution. If the student succeeds in solving the problem, praise him or her on the success and for taking the time to practice with you. If the solution doesn't work out the way the student thought it would, be supportive and empathetic. You and the student can always return to the SODAS method to find another solution.

Problems, Options, Plan

A similar though slightly abbreviated version of SODAS is called **POP**, which stands for **Problem, Options,** and **Plan**. This decision-making method is best suited for younger students or those whose developmental level requires a more simplistic approach. The POP process is similar to SODAS in that you help students clarify what the problem is, identify the options they have for dealing with it, and then follow through on whichever option is chosen. With the POP process, you probably will need to provide more direction or direct guidance because students' life experiences will be more limited, and they will be even less aware of potential options and their consequences.

Both SODAS and POP share two important goals – to help students arrive at sound solutions to their problems and to teach them how to solve problems in a systematic, rational way. You can use these decision-making strategies to empower students to think clearly and make decisions based on sound reasoning. It also helps strengthen your relationships with students. The conversations you have, the listening you do, and the concern and empathy you show all promote and establish trust, which is the foundation of any healthy relationship.

Limitations

Although problem solving gives you and your students a plan for dealing with everyday problems, it's important to understand that SODAS and POP are not cure-alls for every challenge. For example, when trying to teach students a new social skill, preventive teaching strategies (Chapter 11) are more appropriate. Also, when a student struggles with inappropriate behaviors, such as not accepting criticism, not accepting "No" for an answer, or not staying on task, there are other corrective strategies (Chapters 13 and 14) you can use to better address those problems. There may be times when you want to help a student problem solve when he or she is in crisis or out of control, especially if the student is crying or complaining about unfairness. Rather than going through the SODAS process, it's better to focus on regaining the student's attention and cooperation (strategies to help students regain their composure are discussed in Section III). Later, when the student is calm and has fully regained control of his or her behavior, you may (or the student may ask you to) initiate a problem-solving session.

Sometimes, the problems students face – illness or death of a friend or family member, parents' separation or divorce, the break-up of a dating relationship, or suicide ideation – will be too serious for you to address on your own. You may not be comfortable or feel competent enough to discuss these issues alone with the student. In these types of circumstances, you should seek the assistance and support of a school counselor or psychologist, or another qualified professional in the community. Whenever a student talks about taking his or her own life, says he or she is "wishing" for death, or comes to you with any issue that makes you uneasy, contact the student's parents or guardian and a qualified staff member or professional person in the community who can assist the student. (The **Boys Town National Hotline® – 1-800-448-3000** – is staffed by professional counselors 24 hours a day, 7 days a week. Students of any age can call for help with problems of any kind, including bullying, relationships, dating, suicide, etc. Referrals to local services and resources can be made.)

Final Thoughts

When teaching rational problem-solving skills to students, it's best to follow the complete SODAS format. As you go through the process, remember to engage in supportive verbal and nonverbal behaviors that communicate care, concern, and empathy. Learning to problem solve is a complex task, but as mentioned earlier in this chapter, it is a life skill and one that is critical to your students' eventual success.

Because the problem-solving process is so essential, students may earn positive consequences when they demonstrate this skill. Since many students have "solved" their problems in inappropriate ways in the past (talking back, running away, becoming aggressive), it's important to positively reinforce them whenever they come to you and want to discuss a problem.

There are two important distinctions you should be aware of as you teach and guide students in the problem-solving process. First, students should be encouraged to generate their own options to their own problems rather than you always telling them what they should do or what you think is the best solution. Students need to take ownership of their behavior. When they begin to generate alternatives, they are more likely to learn that they do have a certain amount of control over what happens to them. They also are learning critical thinking skills. Second, the emphasis again must be on teaching students the process or skill of how to problem solve rather than on judging the solution itself. Students must be allowed to make mistakes or poor decisions as part of learning how to make the most effective or reasonably "correct" decision.

Aside from formal problem-solving sessions, there are many other types of formal and informal activities that facilitate modeling and direct teaching of the SODAS method. Informally, the content of television programs and events in the news can offer great opportunities to discuss problem solving. When students express their opinions and points of view, you will have many opportunities to encourage them to think, to weigh options, and to discuss the possible ramifications of their views and values.

Even when your students possess the skills necessary to solve problem situations they face, it doesn't guarantee they will use them when confronted with a problem. Here are several factors to keep in mind as you work with your students on the difficult skill of problem solving:

Model problem solving for your students. Whenever appropriate, use SODAS, POP, or other cognitive behavior-management strategies. Talk with your students about situations in which you are using or have used SODAS to work through a problem.

Take time to provide specific teaching in the SODAS process. Assess students' skills on a regular basis and provide follow-up teaching as needed.

Follow up with students. Ask students how well their solutions worked out for them. We recommend using the mnemonic device "SODAS with a Fizz" as a prompt to "Follow up" with students or to remind them to report back on how well they did in trying to resolve their problems.

Praise students whenever they spontaneously use SODAS or POP. Be observant and recognize when students try to solve problems independently. In one classroom we visited, the teacher had set aside a special "Decision Desk," where students could sit and privately fill out a SODAS or POP worksheet when they were frustrated or struggling with a situation. Whenever a student voluntarily sat there and worked through a legitimate problem, the teacher offered words of encouragement and praised the student's initiative and self-management skills.

Promote generalization by encouraging students to use their problem-solving skills outside of the classroom or school setting. Assign homework or provide opportunities to engage in other activities that require your students to use these skills with peers and adults.

Analyzing Behavior:
Behavior Management Theory

The strategies and practices outlined in the previous two chapters empha-sized relationships. Chapter 1 encouraged you to adopt a variety of interper-sonal and instructional techniques to improve your efforts at reaching out and connecting with students. Chapter 2 highlighted how problem-solving skills can empower young people to think more critically and make better choices. Both chapters illustrated how changes in perspective can lead to better out-comes. In this chapter, we look at behavior from the perspective of social learning theory and how the principles of behavior management can reduce or eliminate students' disruptive and inappropriate actions.

The practices advocated throughout this manual represent components of the Boys Town Education Model®, which is rooted in social learning theory. In order to understand and effectively use the basic principles of the theory, you have to consider the various meanings of the word "learned." One commonly held notion is that if a particular behavior is taught, then it is learned. We disagree. From our perspective, a behavior is learned when the learner successfully demonstrates it over time in appropriate settings. For example, when students struggle with a math concept, teachers generally go back and analyze their teaching approach, change it, and teach the concept again. However, when students struggle with appropriate social skills in the classroom, that same review process or reflection doesn't always happen. Some educators mistakenly assume that certain skills have already been taught to and learned by students, even though it is clear from their behavior that the students lack those skills. For whatever reason, the students choose not to demonstrate the skill. But when dealing with behavior issues, teaching doesn't automatically equate to learning. A continuous teaching process that is refined based on a student's progress needs to continue until he or she can successfully demonstrate appropriate behaviors over time.

Defining the ABC, or Three-Term Contingency, Pattern

No behavior occurs in a vacuum. There are events that precede a behavior and events that follow a behavior that influence future occurrences of that behavior. To fully understand the behavior itself, you have to see the larger context (what's going on in the environment prior to the behavior and what occurs following the behavior). It may be helpful for you to think of the ABC, or three-term contingency, pattern this way:

- **A** stands for **antecedents** – the events or conditions present in the environment before a behavior occurs.

- **B** stands for **behavior** – what is done or said by a person.

- **C** stands for **consequences** – the results, outcomes, or effects that follow a behavior.

According to social learning theorists, the universe is a determined, orderly place in which events do not just randomly happen. They happen as a part of a relationship with other events. This relationship is called a **contingency**. Behavior always occurs as a part of a contingency.

Antecedents

The situation or context in which behavior occurs qualifies as the antecedent to that behavior. These conditions or events can be simple or complex, recent or historical. When analyzing the antecedents of a behavior, pay particular attention to who was present, what activities were occurring, the time of day or season of the year, and the location or physical setting.

Each of these alone or in conjunction with one another can set the occasion for particular behaviors to occur. The more you know about the history of a student, the greater your understanding will be of the previous learning that has occurred with him or her. Learning history can play a role in the antecedents of current behavior.

While all the antecedents for a behavior may be complex, a singular, simpler stimulus (or set of stimuli) can also immediately precede a behavior. A doorbell ringing immediately precedes someone standing to answer the door. A student's smiling face first thing in the morning sets the occasion for a greeting. A green light at an intersection precedes a driver's continued pressure on the gas pedal. A student arguing with a teacher after being given an instruction precedes the teacher's action of intervening and teaching the student how to follow an instruction appropriately.

Behavior

Behavior is anything a person does or says that can be directly or indirectly observed (seen, heard, felt, touched, or smelled) and measured. For example, you can observe the behavior of writing numbers on a math assignment directly by watching the action as it occurs, or indirectly, by seeing the physical results of the behavior – a completed math worksheet.

Consequences

Consequences are results, changes, or reactions in the environment that occur after a behavior. Consequences usually occur relatively quickly in a chronological sequence and can alter the probability that the behavior will occur again (Cooper, Heron, & Heward, 2006). Consequences take one of two forms:

1. A new stimulus is presented or added to the environment. For example, a student earns free time on the computer after completing an in-class assignment.

2. An already-present stimulus is terminated or removed from the environment. For example, a student loses the privilege of recess after failing to complete a homework assignment.

Consequences can either increase or decrease the future occurrence rate of a particular behavior. Consequences that increase the likelihood of a behavior repeating itself are considered "reinforcements." When consequences decrease the chances of a behavior reoccurring, they are considered "punishments."

Consequences are either natural or applied. Natural consequences are the typical outcomes of a behavior without any intentional human intervention. For example, scrapes and bruises are the natural consequences of falling down on a cement sidewalk; falling backwards is a natural consequence of leaning back too far in a chair.

Applied consequences for behavior are outcomes that are purposefully arranged. For example, when students engage in appropriate behavior or academic tasks, they can earn privileges (increased computer time, extended recess, etc.). Or, students may lose privileges (choice of seating assignment, loss of free time, etc.) for being disruptive or not completing academic tasks to specifications.

Using the ABC, or Three-Term Contingency, Pattern

Understanding the ABC pattern can give you insight into why a behavior occurs. More importantly, you will be in a better position to help students change their behaviors. Many young people engage in negative classroom behaviors that, if generalized, will isolate them from family, friends, school activities, and their community at large. Due to various socio-cultural realities, some of these youth are dependent on you for help in overcoming their behavioral shortcomings. Using the ABC pattern allows you to promote behavior change in positive, effective, and efficient ways.

Manipulating antecedents, consequences, or both can influence student behavior. One common misconception is that only consequences determine the degree to which behaviors change. While that may often prove to be true, there are times when altering the antecedents is the most effective way to influence behavior. For example, Nidra is a high school junior who struggles to get out of bed in the morning and hits the snooze button repeatedly instead of getting up and making it to school on time. She (or her parents) could alter the antecedent by moving the alarm clock to the other side of her bedroom. This makes it more difficult for her to immediately go back to sleep because she has to get up and walk across the room to hit the snooze button. Since she's already up, it may compel her to stay awake. Another example of changing antecedents in order to change behavior could involve a particular social situation, such as a school pep rally. Behaviors that should occur during a pep rally (cheering, applause, appropriate comments, etc.) can be rehearsed ahead of time and the most relevant behaviors can be pointed out and discussed. Cues and subtle signals that will prompt appropriate behavior at the rally can be explained to the students. In both of those examples, the antecedent conditions have been altered to help achieve a desired behavioral change.

Of course, changing consequences can also produce behavior change. For example, if a student uses inappropriate behaviors (yelling your name, waving arms, etc.) to get your attention, a negative consequence could be the loss of a privilege. This negative consequence motivates the student to use more appropriate behaviors (raising her hand, speaking softly, etc.) the next time she tries to gain your attention. To reinforce this positive behavior, you could reward her with verbal praise or another positive consequence. We'll touch on consequences throughout the book, including the important characteristics that influence their effectiveness in Chapter 8.

For difficult student problems, unique situations, or recurring problems, use the ABC pattern to analyze the situation and come up with solutions. By altering antecedents and adjusting consequences, you can motivate changes in student behavior.

Principles of Behavior

In your learning community, there are a number of consequences that affect student behavior as defined or illustrated by the principles of behavior. These principles are critical when you're trying to affect students' actions and attitudes. Among the approaches you can use are positive and negative reinforcement to increase behavior, and positive and negative punishment to decrease behavior (see the chart on page 44). You also can use generalization and discrimination training. These are processes for teaching appropriate behavior in a variety of contexts and social situations. You also can help students learn to respond to naturally occurring reinforcements through techniques such as extinction, shaping, and fading. Let's look at these principles in more detail.

Positive reinforcement. Positive reinforcement means using consequences immediately after a behavior to increase the likelihood that the behavior will occur again in the future. If the behavior occurs more often or gets stronger, then the behavior was "reinforced" by the consequence. Therefore, if a behavior increases, regardless of what the consequence was, it has been reinforced.

Changing Behavior Through Consequences

	Add	Subtract
To Increase a Behavior	Something Pleasant **(Positive Reinforcement)**	Something Unpleasant **(Negative Reinforcement)**
To Decrease a Behavior	Something Unpleasant **(Positive Punishment)**	Something Pleasant **(Response Cost/ Negative Punishment)**

Positive reinforcement can occur with natural or applied consequences. An example of a natural consequence for positive reinforcement is the feeling of euphoria a high school basketball player gets when she makes a three-point shot at the buzzer to win the game. The crowd goes wild and her teammates give her hugs and high-fives. The results of this public praise will motivate her to continue playing basketball at school. An example of an applied consequence is a teacher's promise to a student that finishing an assignment in 10 minutes will earn him 10 minutes of computer time. When he finishes his assignment on time, he gets to use the computer. This helps motivate the student to complete future assignments in a timely fashion.

Positive reinforcement can help students learn new behaviors or maintain appropriate behaviors. There are several conditions that impact the effectiveness of positive reinforcements, including immediacy and size. We take a closer look at these conditions in Chapter 8, "Understanding and Giving Consequences."

Shaping. Behavioral shaping is defined as the differential reinforcement of successive approximations to a desired behavior (Alberto & Troutman, 2006). In other words, shaping encourages the gradual development of a new behavior by continually reinforcing small improvements or steps toward that targeted behavior or goal. Rather than expecting a new behavior to occur exactly the way you taught it, you reinforce any behavior that closely resembles the goal. Differential reinforcement means that one behavior is reinforced while another behavior that was previously displayed is not. Both behaviors are similar or related (meaning they come from the same response class.).

The chart on page 46 illustrates a shaping process and how differential reinforcement is the key principle being used. In the example, the shaping process is designed to help a student who never sits up straight at his desk and slouches down so low that his backside is off or nearly off the desk seat. This step-by-step training progression begins by reinforcing the specific behavior or action of having the student keep his seat on the desk chair. When that behavior is established, having the student move his backside closer to the back of the desk chair is reinforced. At this point, you no longer reinforce the behavior of keeping his seat on the desk chair. Next, you reinforce the student for having his lower back touching the back of the desk chair while not reinforcing the previous behaviors. This shaping process continues until he achieves the final goal of sitting upright at his desk.

A successive approximation to a desired behavior is an action that is either part of the goal behavior or a combination of successive steps that lead to the goal behavior. For example, if the goal is to get Lara to wear her glasses all day at school, the successive approximations might look like this: She picks up her glasses, puts them on, wears them for one class period, wears them for half a day, etc., until she finally achieves the stated goal.

The advantages of behavioral shaping include:

1. It is a positive procedure because reinforcement is delivered consistently as the student moves closer to the ultimate goal.

2. It can be used to teach new behaviors. Because shaping is a gradual process, the end goal or desired behavior is always in sight.

Differential Reinforcement

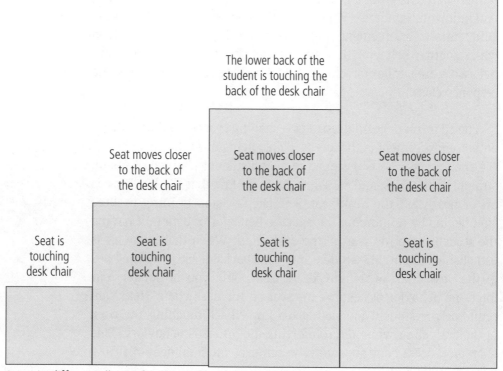

Sitting upright in the desk

The lower back of the
student is touching the
back of the desk chair

Seat moves closer
to the back of
the desk chair

Seat moves closer
to the back of
the desk chair

Seat moves closer
to the back of
the desk chair

Seat is
touching
desk chair

Seat is
touching
desk chair

Seat is
touching
desk chair

Seat is
touching
desk chair

Steps in differentially reinforcing sitting upright; shaded portion includes behaviors no longer reinforced as the process moves forward.

The disadvantages of behavioral shaping include:

1. It is a time-consuming process. Extended training with the student may be necessary before the final goal is met.

2. Progress does not always go easily from one behavior to the next. There can be setbacks, or the progression can be interrupted. The student's behavior may become erratic, with considerable time lapses between moments of progress. Certain steps may need to be further dissected into even smaller steps so that smaller approximations can be mastered. This requires considerable effort and monitoring in order to detect any subtle indications that the next step in the sequence has been performed.

3. Because monitoring is time consuming, it sometimes does not occur. This can make the whole shaping procedure ineffective and inefficient.

Here are several guidelines that can make a behavioral shaping program more effective and efficient:

1. Select a specific behavior goal. The more behaviorally specific you can be, the greater the likelihood of success.

2. Decide the criteria for success. Some common criteria for success may include the rate, frequency, percentage, magnitude, and duration of behavior. These should be specified so you know whether the goal has been achieved.

3. Conduct a behavioral or task analysis of the goal behavior. What steps are necessary and in what sequence do they need to be performed for the goal to be attained?

4. Identify the first behavior to reinforce. The behavior should already occur at some minimal level and be similar to or related to the goal behavior. The first behavior reinforced already has a direct link to the goal behavior, which moves the student closer to attaining the goal.

5. Proceed in gradual steps. This is critical for success. The student's approximation of the goal dictates how quickly the goal is attained. Do not move ahead until a step is achieved or learned by the student.

6. Continue reinforcement when a desired behavior is achieved. If reinforcement is not continued, the behavior will be lost and the student's behavior will regress. Reinforce the behavior until the goal criterion is met and a schedule of reinforcement is established.

7. When at all possible, link the behavior to other behaviors that will help the student be more productive at school and in other areas of his or her life.

Fading. Fading refers to the gradual removal of antecedent prompts and cues so that naturally occurring events prompt the desired behavior. Here is an example of how fading can be used in the classroom: One of your students loses a privilege each time she doesn't pay attention. As a prompt to pay attention, you start using a physical gesture such as looking directly at her and then putting your finger to your eyes. Once the student is consistently responding to your prompt, you can begin to use the prompt less often. The goal is to have the student respond with little or no prompting.

Negative reinforcement. Negative reinforcement is taking away something unpleasant immediately following a behavior in order to increase the frequency of that behavior in the future. Like positive reinforcement, negative reinforcement, by definition, increases the frequency of a target behavior.

A classroom example of negative reinforcement is when a teacher tells his or her students that they will not have any homework if they work hard on their in-class assignments. The avoidance of homework is the prime motivator for their performance on that task.

Negative reinforcement can prove to be a powerful motivating force for students. It's also effective whenever students are learning new skills. The possibility that they may lose enjoyable privileges such as recess, free time, or extended computer time encourages them to use skills and engage in appropriate behaviors because they don't want to lose access to those perks.

There are two contingencies related to negative reinforcement that should be mentioned. They are escape/escape and avoidance/avoidance (Cooper, Heron, & Heward, 1987). Escape/escape stops a negative behavior. For example, two girls call each other names and yell at each other. You reprimand them by telling the girls to stop bickering. The back-and-forth between the students stops momentarily. As a result, you are negatively reinforced for using reprimands because it stopped the bickering.

Avoidance/avoidance occurs when a student uses a behavior in order to avoid rather than improve or change a problem situation. For example, a student might follow your instructions in order to avoid being sent to the office, or sit directly behind the bus driver to avoid being teased by other kids on the bus. In each situation, the student is escaping a negative stimulus.

Unintended Outcomes

Using negative reinforcement is not without potential pitfalls. Sometimes, negative behaviors can be unintentionally reinforced. Here is a situation that shows how negative reinforcement can lead to a negative outcome:

Marco is a high school freshman who struggles with reading. Once a month in English class, students take turns reading aloud from a novel. Marco hates this activity because he reads slower than his classmates and often needs help pronouncing words. Marco knows his teacher will send him to the office if he curses in class. So, to avoid the embarrassment of reading aloud, Marco tells the teacher he thinks the novel is "s–" and reading out loud is "f–ing stupid."

Marco is sent to the office. As a result, he avoids the unpleasant experience of reading in class. The teacher, too, is glad Marco is gone. Both have been negatively reinforced. The next time Marco is called on to read, he most likely will curse or act out so he can get out of class, and the teacher will oblige, thus reinforcing his negative behavior.

When using negative reinforcement, make sure you reinforce positive behaviors, not negative ones. Remember, the goal is to increase the student's use of whatever positive behavior you're targeting. Also, be mindful of the consequences you use. Whether positive or negative, they should not inadvertently or unintentionally reinforce inappropriate behaviors.

Positive punishment. To most people, the term "punishment" elicits images of physical or psychological pain that follows a particular behavior. Generally, a person would think that a child who was spanked after running into the street was punished for that behavior. However, the definition of punishment, as a principle of behavior, is the application of an aversive stimulus (following a behavior) that decreases the likelihood that the behavior will occur again. If the child does not run into the street again, then the spanking could be called positive punishment. However, if the spanking does not decrease the behavior, then it would not be considered punishment.

There are unconditioned and conditioned aversive stimuli. A stimulus that has not previously been experienced is an unconditioned aversive stimulus. For example, a teacher might have music playing in the background whenever students work independently. When the students' conversations get too loud, he might turn up the sound so it's blaring, which causes the students to quiet down as they try to figure out what just happened.

A conditioned aversive stimulus is an event that is initially perceived as neutral, but becomes aversive in nature when it is repeatedly paired with an unconditioned aversive stimulus. An example is the word "No." It is not inherently aversive. However, continually pairing it with a loud, harsh voice tone can make "No" become aversive to students in a classroom.

Three things must happen in order for something to be defined as punishment:

1.   A behavior must be displayed.

2.   The behavior must be followed by an aversive stimulus.

3.   That stimulus alone must decrease the probability that the behavior will occur in the future.

While it is important to know what positive punishment is, we do not recommend its use because it has many negative side effects. These include:

1.   **The punisher is negatively reinforced.** The person delivering the punishment is negatively reinforced because the behavior ceases. So a teacher may be more likely to use the same

procedure in the future instead of trying something that is less punishing or harmful to the teacher-student relationship.

2. **The student becomes emotional or aggressive.** The student may attack, escape, or become physically aggressive in an effort to stop the punishment.

3. **Avoidance and escape.** Avoidance of the punisher can take a literal sense when students avoid the actual punishment or the place they were punished. For example, a student who is punished for being late for class may not go to class. Avoidance and escape behaviors also can occur in a non-literal sense. For example, a student might escape punishing environments by taking drugs and alcohol, or by "tuning out" (Cooper, Heron, & Heward, 1987).

4. **Negative modeling.** If you punish a child for a behavior, the child will most likely imitate the punishment. Modeling punitive forms of behavior may negate the positive effects of your teaching.

5. **Unpredictability.** Side effects of punishment may be difficult to predict prior to implementing an intervention strategy. Whenever you use an aversive stimulus, you should be aware of the potential effects and have an alternate plan for handling the situation.

Response cost/Negative punishment. Response cost is a form of punishment in which a specific amount of reinforcement is lost as a result of an inappropriate behavior (see p. 44). As punishment, this decreases the probability that a behavior will occur again. A student losing part of his free time for not following your instructions or a student losing privileges because she did not complete her homework are examples of response cost.

There are three desirable aspects of using response cost:

1. Similar to other forms of punishment, response cost usually produces a moderate-to-rapid decrease in behavior. Results of this procedure are apparent after a reasonable trial period, usually three to five days (Cooper, Heron, & Heward, 1987).

2. Response cost is a convenient procedure to use in the classroom. Many studies have shown a decrease in negative classroom behavior as a result of using these procedures.

3. Response cost can be combined with other behavioral procedures in a comprehensive behavior-change strategy. In the Boys Town Education Model®, response cost is combined with the "fair pair" rule developed by White and Haring (1980). This rule suggests that teachers reinforce one or more alternatives for every behavior targeted for reduction. In other words, teach prosocial alternatives to any behavioral mistake. The combination of positive reinforcement and response cost helps to motivate students to replace their misbehaviors with more appropriate behaviors.

Like positive reinforcement, conditions such as immediacy and size (see Chapter 8) affect response cost. You must take these into account in order to maximize the effectiveness of your consequences.

Extinction. Extinction is a procedure in which you stop or withhold a reinforcement that maintains or encourages inappropriate behavior. Put another way, extinction consists of ignoring a behavior to make it "go away."

According to Alberto and Troutman (2006), extinction can be used in the classroom to diminish a student's inappropriate behavior, especially any behavior that is reinforced or encouraged by teacher attention. Some young people relish attention, even when that attention is negative or harsh. Students who misbehave in the classroom typically are noticed by the teacher and "find such attention positively reinforcing" (p. 272). For those students, ignoring their minor misbehaviors may be an effective and convenient way to stop it. Take this situation for example: Dara taps her pencil on her desk. The noise is distracting, so you tell her to stop tapping her pencil. She obliges. Moments later, however, she starts again. This time you ignore the behavior. You realize Dara's just trying to elicit a response from you; you also realize that this behavior is not worth your time or attention. Eventually, Dara stops tapping her pencil because it did not produce the reaction she had hoped for.

Obviously, in a classroom situation, ignoring inappropriate behavior is difficult and may not be a viable option. If Dara continued to tap her pencil, engaged in other distracting behaviors, or escalated her behavior, then extinction isn't working. Other corrective strategies (highlighted in Chapter 13) are required to fix this situation. That's why extinction should be used cautiously. While it can be an effective strategy for stopping minor or nuisance behaviors – toe tapping, pencil tapping, loud sighing – that are more distracting than disruptive, it doesn't work with all students or in all circumstances.

If adult attention is reinforcing a student's inappropriate behavior, and if extinction is going to be used to correct the behavior or is part of a larger behavior intervention plan, then everyone who is helping the student – behavior intervention specialists, support staff, teachers, coaches, administrators, and parents – must understand and be aware of the strategy. Otherwise it's likely to be misused and ineffective.

Generalization. Generalization refers to a student's ability to demonstrate appropriate skills and behaviors in a variety of different settings. For example, skills learned in a classroom can be generalized to environments outside the classroom. This principle of behavior means that each skill does not have to be taught in each new environment where it could be used. Generalization can be promoted by having students thoroughly practice each skill and by conducting the practice under conditions that simulate the student's real environments (home, other classrooms, sports practices, recreation areas, etc.). You can effectively promote generalization by monitoring how students behave in different situations. This feedback, whether it comes through firsthand or secondhand observations, creates opportunities for you to reinforce students for generalizing appropriate behaviors in new and different environments.

Discrimination. Discrimination means that changes in the antecedent conditions produce changes in behavior. In this sense, discrimination is the opposite of generalization. Discrimination means that a behavior is used only under certain circumstances but not under other, different circumstances. For example, if a student uses slang with his friends but uses proper grammar when talking with you, he has appropriately discriminated between those two different contexts. Similarly, aggression that is appropriate in an athletic contest is not appropriate in the classroom.

Much of the teaching you do not only helps students learn new skills, but also teaches them where and under what conditions certain behaviors are appropriate. Teaching youth behavioral discrimination is crucial. They must learn to recognize the environmental cues that call for different sets of behavior. This skill is also called "code switching," which we explain in more detail in Chapter 11.

Final Thoughts

The principles of behavior described in this chapter are reflected in the teaching strategies and classroom management methods that define our Well-Managed Schools practices. This abbreviated look at social learning theory is designed to give you a deeper understanding of why we advocate certain practices and how those practices can motivate behavior change. By learning how these principles can be applied in your learning community, you can reduce disruptive behaviors while helping students enjoy success in other areas of life.

Observing and Describing Behavior

Joaquin and Aidan were best buddies at Eisenhower High, a sprawling suburban school. Both boys had the same mid-day schedule on Fridays – lunch at 11:30 followed by Mr. De LaCruz's calculus class at 12:15. On this particular Friday, the boys were more than a little excited because it was the last day of class before an extended weekend.

During their lunch period, Joaquin and Aidan goofed off with several friends. After the bell rang, they continued horsing around as they walked to class. The boys traded punches to the arm, tripped unsuspecting freshmen walking in front of them, catcalled girls who passed by, and generally harassed anyone they met whom they did not know or like. As they strutted into Mr. De LaCruz's classroom, Aidan punctuated their rowdiness with a loud belch. The sophomoric gesture was met with laughs by his fellow students, but Aidan's teacher only offered an icy stare.

Joaquin and Aidan took their seats across from each other in the back row. When Joaquin wasn't looking, Aidan leaned over and punched him in the arm. Joaquin yelped, "Oww!" Mr. De LaCruz looked at the boys and said, "Knock it off you two." Then he turned his back to the class and continued writing differentiation formulas on the blackboard. Aidan looked at Joaquin and mockingly mimicked the teacher's reprimand. Both boys chuckled, drawing everyone's attention again, including Mr. De LaCruz's. "Hey! I thought I told you to knock it off. Just stop it!"

The boys got back on task – but only momentarily. Soon, Aidan was using his feet to push the desk in front of him. He kicked the backrest too, just to aggravate the boy who sat there. Joaquin laughed at Aidan's antics and the two of them snickered.

Mr. De LaCruz had heard enough and lost his patience. He directed his frustration at Aidan.

"Why are you disrespecting me, or are you just being stupid to impress your friend?" shouted Mr. De LaCruz.

Aidan retorted, "I'm not stupid."

"Be quiet, or I will send you to the office," a frustrated Mr. De LaCruz said as he pointed his finger at Aidan.

"Go ahead and send me to the office. I don't care. It's better than sitting in your lame class," mumbled Aidan.

"If that's what you want, that's what you'll get. Go to the office now. And if I hear another peep out of you Joaquin, you will join him. Understood?" said Mr. De LaCruz.

Aidan left the room. Joaquin sat silently.

In the end, Aidan's inability or unwillingness to follow the teacher's instructions led him down a path to the principal's office. Aidan made several poor choices, but there were a number of other factors that conspired against him. In the previous chapter, we discussed the ABC's of behavior. In this example, the antecedents included the time (first period after lunch on a Friday before a long weekend), seating arrangement (both friends sat side by side in the back row), and previous events (no consequences for harassing others in the hallway or for the crude noise made in class). All of these factors played a role in Aidan's escalating misbehaviors. It was unfortunate so many behavioral problems were missed or ignored in the hallway. The in-class disruptions might never have happened had there been an earlier intervention. Even so, when Aidan continued to act out in the classroom, the intervention efforts that did occur were doomed to fail because Mr. De LaCruz's responses were loaded with too many ambiguities and accusations.

Repeating phrases like "Knock it off" does little to help a student understand exactly what it is you want him or her to stop doing, even when you think it's obvious. And "Knock it off" doesn't tell a student what he or she should do instead. Also, making assumptions about the personal motives for a student's misbehavior, then sharing that opinion with him or her, is usually counterproductive and often unnecessary. If your assumption is wrong, the student may become more agitated or emotional and perceive you as heavy-handed, unfair, and judgmental. Then it becomes very difficult to develop or maintain any type of positive relationship with the student. And even if you're right about the motive, tossing it back at the student may only infuriate him or her more, which makes coming to any kind of resolution more difficult and time consuming.

In later chapters, we will outline specific strategies and teaching techniques for shaping student behavior in positive directions. The success of these methods and the degree to which you can create a healthy, supportive environment for all students hinges on how well you can do what Mr. De LaCruz could not – observe and describe behavior.

Regardless of whether you're offering praise to a student who's staying on task, giving a consequence to a student who isn't following instructions, or conferencing with the parents of a disruptive student, these interactions require the ability to accurately and objectively describe what happened or is happening. Without that skill, it's much more difficult to get the cooperation you need or the behavioral change you desire. Anyone can witness an event or interaction and describe what went on. But it takes practice and effort to frame the situation in language that is clear, concise, and nonjudgmental. Observing and describing behavior is a professional skill you need because it forms the foundation or starting point for nearly all the teaching efforts and interactions we advocate in this book.

Observing Behavior

The goal of observing and describing behavior is to accurately verbalize what is happening in a given situation. The best descriptions are those that mirror a person's behavior so clearly that the behavior could be repeated or re-enacted by someone who hadn't observed the behavior firsthand.

The first step in observing and describing any behavior is to watch and listen carefully. Determine who was involved in the situation and pay particular attention to these details:

What the student is doing. Look at both large and small body movements, such as running, walking, kicking, throwing, hand gestures, and body posture.

The student's facial expressions. Look for smiles, scowls, grimaces, stares, eye rolling, or eye contact. These nonverbal cues often can reveal the student's real feelings.

What the student is saying. Listen carefully to specific words and how they are said. Voice tone and inflection can sometimes be better indicators of what a youth is feeling than the words that are uttered. Also notice giggles, groans, moans, or sighs.

The frequency, intensity, and duration of behavior. These characteristics often determine whether a behavior is appropriate or inappropriate. Monitor whether the behavior occurs too frequently or not frequently enough, whether it escalates in intensity, and whether it lasts too long or not long enough.

When and where the behavior occurs. What events and circumstances happen before the behavior takes place? What time of day does it occur and where does it take place? For example, laughing with a friend in the hallway may be appropriate; laughing with a friend during study hall may be inappropriate.

The absence of behavior. Was there a behavior that should have occurred but did not? For example, did the student fail to look at another person during a conversation, or not answer a question when asked, or fail to raise his or her hand before speaking in class? In the example with Aidan, he failed to offer any apology for burping in class.

Describing Behavior

After closely observing behaviors, begin forming a mental picture of what occurred – almost like an instant replay of the behavior. Your goal is to describe what happened as accurately as possible.

Concentrate solely on what behaviors occurred. An accurate picture of the situation is necessary before any successful intervention can be attempted. Avoid making any judgments about a student's intentions or motives. Instead focus on the following:

Specificity. Avoid using adjectives that are general or vague. You may feel that a student has a "bad attitude," but what behaviors did the student engage in that gave you this impression? Similarly, telling a student "Good job" may indicate general satisfaction, but what specifically was good about it? The goal of being specific is to give students messages that are easily understood and convey exactly what you mean. A "good job" may be more accurately described as "using complete sentences on an essay test," "completing a difficult classroom assignment on time," or "putting all supplies where they belong without being prompted." The more specific you are, the better the student understands, thereby improving the likelihood that positive behaviors will be repeated or negative behaviors will stop. Specificity is especially important when working with students who struggle with certain skills.

DESCRIBING BEHAVIOR

When describing
a student's behavior,
make your descriptions:

- Specific
- Concrete (behaviorally specific)
- Objective

Concrete actions. Break behaviors down into specific components. Telling a student he or she is "antisocial," "rude," or "disrespectful," for example, has no value if the student can't make the connection between those abstract concepts and the concrete actions that define them. Most students, regardless of age, need more clarity, not less. You can clarify a problem by using more descriptive phrasing, such as "not responding when spoken to," "not participating in study groups with other students," "not engaging in extracurricular activities," and so on. By focusing on observable actions rather than indefinable labels, you give the student specific areas where he or she can learn new social skills to overcome or improve a behavioral weakness.

Objectivity. Judgmental terms or labels can harm a relationship by damaging a student's self-esteem or triggering an emotional reaction. Terms like "stupid," "bad," and "terrible" should be avoided. Also, being objective means you have to keep any negative emotions you're feeling under control. (The dangers of reacting emotionally to problem behaviors are discussed in Section III.) Concentrate on us-

Be Descriptive, Not Ambiguous

The following examples compare vague descriptions of students' behavior to specific descriptions of the same situation (note how much more instructive and helpful the specific descriptions are for students):

[DESCRIPTION OF AN INAPPROPRIATE BEHAVIOR]

VAGUE   "Stephen, you were rude to Marcel."

SPECIFIC   "Stephen, just now when Marcel asked for your assistance in putting books back on the shelf, you-sighed, rolled your eyes, and didn't say anything to let him know you would help out."

[A PRAISE STATEMENT]

VAGUE   "Emily, you wrote a really good story for this English assignment."

SPECIFIC   "Awesome job of writing, Emily! You used complete sentences, and all your words were spelled correctly. The issue of immigration is very timely, and your analysis was thoughtful and passionate."

[DESCRIPTION OF AN APPROPRIATE BEHAVIOR]

VAGUE   "That was real nice of you, Da' Quan."

SPECIFIC   "When I asked for a volunteer, you immediately raised your hand and offered to help. You smiled, made eye contact, and used a pleasant voice, Da' Quan, which shows me you're glad to volunteer."

ing a calm, matter-of-fact approach when describing behavior. When you can maintain your objectivity, students will be more willing to accept your feedback and be more likely to see you as someone who is concerned, pleasant, and fair. For example, instead of saying, "You disrespected me," it would be better to use a more behaviorally specific response, such as, "You pushed the desk with your feet, kicked the back of the chair, and continued to laugh."

When describing verbal behavior, use your discretion to decide whether or not you should repeat exactly what a student said. If a student is swearing, using crude language, or repeating an inappropriate statement, it's usually better to begin your description with "You said something like…," and then paraphrase what the student said. Keep in mind that it can be difficult to remember verbatim what was said, so paraphrasing a student's remarks may help you avoid attributing words to a student that he or she never uttered. Also, repeating inappropriate language, even in this context, may set a bad example (negative modeling) and be misinterpreted by some students.

The purpose of specifically yet carefully describing verbal behavior is to help you remain objective and keep the emphasis on observable events and actions.

When to Observe and Describe Behavior

Naturally, observing and describing behaviors is an ongoing process whenever you are working with students. However, there are times when you will want to zero in on certain behaviors. These times include:

When a student's behavior is inappropriate. This could include any form of misbehavior or problem behavior, such as not following an instruction, arguing, or complaining. There may be times when a student engages in many inappropriate behaviors at once. Rather than going on and on about each problem, point out the most overt or obvious behaviors and move on. Students are less likely to tune you out or overreact and escalate their behaviors if you keep your comments brief and specific. (We will talk more about effective corrective responses to problem behaviors in Chapters 13 and 14.)

When a student's behavior is particularly appropriate. This is a special time to "catch 'em being good" – to point out behaviors that you want to see repeated. Too often, we get so focused on dealing with problem behaviors that we forget or neglect the positive things students do. (Using praise to reinforce and encourage appropriate behavior is discussed in Chapter 12.) Emphasizing the things your students do correctly is a great way to develop better relationships with them and motivate them to continue taking positive steps.

When you want to teach a new skill. Describing new behaviors helps students learn quicker and progress through academic and social curricula more efficiently. Accurately describing what was done, both correctly and incorrectly, gives students valuable feedback on their performance and helps them internalize the skill you are teaching. (In Chapter 11, we examine the social skills you may need to teach students if you're going to sustain a positive learning environment.)

Final Thoughts

Observing behaviors and accurately describing them in language that is specific, objective, and concrete is essential if students are ever going to understand your expectations. While this may sound easy enough to do, it requires concentration and effort. When you are frustrated or confronted by an emotionally intense youth, the heat of the moment may cause you to say something regrettable or use words that further antagonize or anger the student. It might also cause you to lecture or go on and on to the point the student tunes you out (brevity is best). In such moments, it's important to think about your ultimate goal and objective: You want to empower students with the knowledge and skills they need to overcome their behavioral mistakes, not shame them into blind obedience or reinforce their feelings of failure and hopelessness.

Providing Reasons:
How to Link Behavior to Results

Every teacher who ever had Drew as a student felt the same way: The boy had a mouth on him that drove everyone to distraction. Drew was a bright kid, but his mouth was always in motion. He had something to say about everything and everyone. Unfortunately, much of what he said was annoying, even antagonistic. If someone dropped a pencil, he'd call out, "Klutz!" If someone said the wrong answer aloud, he'd snicker or make a sound like a buzzer. If a teacher stumbled over her words, he'd say, "Try again." His smart remarks were so constant, few of his classmates could stand to sit next to him. No one wanted to be his lab partner. No one wanted him in their work group. On days when he was absent, the whole class felt a sense of relief. Drew's incessant commentary was a drag. Still, he never said anything so outrageous that it warranted a trip to the office. Nonetheless, his behavior was problematic enough that it needed to be addressed.

In this chapter, we look at how you can use rationales to motivate students like Drew to alter their behavior. (Additional preventive strategies, including creating classroom rules, teaching social skills, and using consequences, are discussed in Section II.) A rationale, by definition, is a fundamental reason. In the classroom, you can use rationales to help students understand the cognitive link between their behavior and the various consequences that may result (Downs, Black, & Kutsick, 1985). Rationales also serve to remind students that they, not someone or something else, control and are responsible for their behavior.

Many young people struggle with cause-and-effect relationships, especially as they relate to their personal behavior. In 1974, D.S. Eitzen conducted a survey of the attitudes of predelinquent and delinquent adolescents and found that they didn't understand that their behavior determines what happens to them. Instead, they often see themselves as "victims of fate," or blame other people for their problems. For example, a student who gets caught cheating on a test and consequently suffers a failing grade may blame the teacher for catching him rather than realizing the consequence was a logical outcome of his behavior.

People use rationales every day to convince themselves or others of the benefits or drawbacks of maintaining or changing a behavior. For example, a coach gets his players to practice hard by telling them that they will perform better during games, increasing their chances of winning (the rationale). A doctor tells her patient he could add years to his life (the rationale) if he quits smoking. A worker convinces himself to take on extra projects at work in hopes that his boss might notice and consider him for a promotion (the rationale).

In the classroom, a rationale sounds and works in the same way. It is a statement that describes the possible benefits or negative consequences a student might receive for engaging in a certain behavior. For example, this is a rationale Drew's teacher used with him when correcting his behavior:

"When you constantly talk over your classmates and draw attention to their mistakes, they don't want to be around you, which means you'll end up doing group assignments on your own – in the office – instead of working with everyone else in the lab."

Was that a good enough reason to motivate Drew to change his behavior? The teacher didn't think so. But did it work? Yes. Why? The teacher used a rationale that meant something to Drew. She could have told him how his behavior was bothersome and disruptive to everyone (we call this a "concern-for-others" rationale), but getting under people's skin was Drew's motivation. Talking about how his behavior affected others would have been meaningless. Instead, Drew's teacher pointed out how his behavior might isolate him from the class. Drew was a kid who wanted to be where the action was, so the realization that he could get isolated from the group if he didn't tone down his behavior was very meaningful to him.

When rationales don't mean anything to a young person, then it doesn't matter how good you think the rationale sounds or how much sense you think it makes. Good rationales are the ones that work, and the ones that work have meaning to the student. It will be up to you to determine what reasons will have the greatest effect and make the most sense to a particular student. To do that, you have to consider his or her developmental level, personal needs or wants, and the overall context of the situation. If one rationale doesn't work, try another. You have options.

Types of Rationales

Rationales fall into three main categories:

- Benefits to self

- Negative outcomes

- Concern for others

A **benefits-to-self rationale** answers the questions of "What's in it for me?" or "How can it help me?" For example, a benefit statement might be, "When you can get a teacher's attention appropriately, you'll be more likely to get the help you need quickly and possibly finish your work faster." A rationale for avoiding inappropriate behavior might sound like, "When you don't tease others, they're more likely to want to be around you and include you in games or activities." Both examples point out a potential gain or benefit to the student. Benefit rationales tend to be the most positive or meaningful to students, especially those who are less developmentally mature.

Going back to Drew's situation, the teacher used a rationale that identified a potentially negative outcome. A benefit-oriented rationale would sound something like this: "Drew, when you concentrate on your task and refrain from making negative comments about other people's work, you show respect and can continue to stay in the lab with your classmates."

By identifying a student's goals and tailoring rationales to match those goals, you can influence his or her behavior. Here is another example: If you have a student who is motivated to improve her grades, you might provide the rationale that accepting (and implementing) feedback about assignments could help her master the content and earn higher grades on tests or future assignments. For a student whose immediate goal is to drop out of school as soon as possible, such a rationale is pointless. With a disconnected student, rationales that emphasize employment prospects or daily living issues are more likely to resonate.

A **negative outcomes rationale** states the potential negative outcomes associated with inappropriate behavior. Examples include: "When you don't turn assignments in, you get further behind, your grade drops, and you could even fail the class," or "If you argue when you're being corrected, you may not get the help you need and may repeat the same mistakes," or "If you don't smile and return someone's greeting, the person may think you're rude and not want to be your friend."

For many people, talking up the negative seems easier to do than emphasizing the positive. But you'll want to avoid falling into the trap of using negative reasons more often than positive ones with your students. If you point out only the negative, your rationales can start to sound a lot like warnings or threats. Rationales are not threats and shouldn't be used that way. They should emphasize opportunities for success, and your students need to hear how they can succeed. There may be many kids in your classroom who are all too familiar with punishment and failure. Pointing out how they might fail yet again can be demoralizing.

A **concern-for-others rationale** describes the effects a child's behavior may have on other people. This type of rationale encourages young people to be other-centered as opposed to self-centered. Examples include: "When you call out to get a teacher's attention, you disturb others who are trying to complete their assignments," or "When you tease other students, they may take you seriously and their feelings could be hurt." Again, using the example of Drew, a concern-for-others rationale might be, "When you are part of the group, you can help others learn and understand the information shared in the lab."

Many students, because of age, developmental level, or personal needs, are unable to consider the rights, feelings, or wants of others. Therefore, gradually introducing this type of rationale into the teaching process, especially when a student is showing behavioral gains, may be the most effective approach. The ultimate goal is to teach all of your students to think about what effect their behavior has on the class and the school.

Benefits of Rationales

Rationales can do more than help young people connect the dots between behaviors and consequences. They also can improve the behavior and culture of your classroom. Here's how:

- When students know the reasons why they should follow rules or respond to requests, they're more likely to comply.

- When students hear rationales, they are more likely to understand that what you are saying has relevance. This helps them see you as someone who is fair because you focus on behavior, not their personal shortcomings.

- When you point out how your students' behaviors affect others, you help them become more other-centered. By helping students see beyond their own self-interests, you're promoting healthy values like respect and empathy.

- When you and other staff members use rationales, you have an opportunity to teach character issues and reinforce concepts like fairness, caring, responsibility, and trustworthiness.

- When you give rationales, your students see that you care. This is an important element in building positive relationships with them. The more positive the relationship, the easier teaching is for you and learning is for them.

Components of Rationales

Effective rationales have these five characteristics:

1. **They apply to natural or logical consequences.** Pointing out consequences that naturally or logically occur as a result of a behavior is ideal. Natural consequences are those that you would expect to happen as a result of the behavior. They typ-

ically occur without human intervention and are outside a student's direct control. Using a natural consequence might sound something like this: "If you run down the hallway, you could slip and hurt yourself," or "If you tip back in your chair, you might fall backward and hit your head."

Logical consequences, on the other hand, are linked to behavior but are determined more by a student's actions or others interacting with the student. Using a logical consequence might sound like this: "When you greet a classmate with a smile and say 'Hello,' he is more likely to want to spend time with you and be your friend," or "If you prepare for a test by studying over a period of time, rather than waiting until the night before, you'll probably earn a higher grade."

2. **They are personal to the youth.** Rationales need to be geared to the individual interests of each student. To do this, you must observe and talk with students to find out their interests, favorite activities, and likes and dislikes. The better your relationships are with your students, the easier it is to individualize your rationales. For example, if you know an eighth-grade student enjoys playing basketball and hopes to play on the high school team next year, you might formulate rationales to help her understand the importance of following instructions and accepting criticisms. This may include taking criticism from the coach, accepting a referee's call, or listening to the coach during practices.

3. **They are specific and brief.** You should be brief and to the point when providing a rationale, and avoid trying to convince the student with numerous reasons. Long explanations can be confusing. You're more likely to keep a student's attention when you keep it brief and specific. Even if the tone of the rationale is positive, a lengthy explanation will be perceived as lecturing and punishing. Usually, one good rationale is enough to accomplish the goal of connecting the student's behavior to its outcome.

4. **They are believable and short-term.** Rationales are more effective when immediate, rather than long-term, consequences are emphasized. An effective rationale for following instructions without arguing might be, "It's more likely

you'll get your work finished or complete your assignment if you don't waste time arguing." Pointing out this short-term, believable consequence is generally preferable to using a remote consequence such as, "When you have a job someday, you will be more likely to get promoted or get a raise if you can follow instructions."

Rationales also must be believable, which means they must be age-appropriate and personalized. For example, you might tell a 9-year-old who enjoys recess, "Putting your things away when I tell you instead of waiting for the bell to ring means you will have all of recess time to play." For a college-bound 17-year-old, a pertinent rationale may be, "If you study hard and do well on your college entrance exams, you might earn a scholarship, which will make paying for college a lot easier."

5. **They are developmentally appropriate.** Rationales that describe short-term, believable consequences are generally the most meaningful for students, especially for those who struggle with social skills or are less developmentally mature.

   However, as students mature and begin to internalize the gains they've made, it's important to use rationales that point out long-term consequences that include statements of concern for others. Long-term rationales point out more general consequences related to a student's behavior. They emphasize what will occur at some point in the more distant future. It is important for students to understand how their behavior may affect their employment, their ability to take care of themselves, and their capacity to develop and maintain relationships. For example, a long-term rationale that could be used when teaching a high school student how to accept criticism might deal with the teen's ability in the future to get along with a spouse or keep a job. Similarly, you need to provide rationales that point out how a student's behavior affects others. Students need to understand that their behavior leaves an impression on others, and that those impressions reflect on them and everyone in the school. For example, a concern-for-others rationale for not getting into fights at a local mall with youth from a rival school would be: "The stores may ask all students to leave the mall because of the behavior of just a few kids." Rationales can point out how the behavior of each child affects others, and how it can benefit or harm other students as well as the school's reputation.

When to Use Rationales

Rationales can be used any time teaching occurs. Rationales make learning more relevant and meaningful to students because they establish a purpose or reason for the learning.

During the course of a day, there will be numerous informal occasions for you to provide rationales. Students may ask your opinion or you may offer advice or a point of view. Including rationales at every opportunity is extremely helpful. Here are situations that provide opportunities to use rationales:

- **When teaching skills and academic concepts.** Rationales should be used in all phases of teaching as a way to establish the relevance of the material to real-life situations or future or past learning. When students are told why specific information is being studied, they demonstrate greater understanding and satisfaction about why they should learn what they are asked to learn (Porter & Brophy, 1988).

  When you're introducing a new social skill during Planned Teaching (discussed in Chapter 11), rationales help students understand why they should learn the skill. Rationales also help reinforce the use of appropriate social skills and provide reasons why students should continue to engage in positive behaviors. Rationales are appropriate anytime, especially when you use Effective Praise (discussed in Chapter 12).

  Rationales are extremely important when correcting problem behaviors, too. Explaining why a student should change a particular behavior and emphasizing the benefits of doing so will help the student realize the cause-effect relationship between the behavior and its outcomes. Understanding this relationship empowers students by helping them learn how to take control of their own behaviors.

- **Whenever disagreements occur between you and your students**. Stating why you disagree gives your students a chance to "buy into" or at least understand your point of view. Your students may also see you as more open-minded and fair. Providing a rationale also models appropriate or desired behavior to students.

- **During problem-solving situations.** When you are helping students generate potential solutions to problems, providing rationales helps them evaluate their options. Rationales can help students make better decisions by considering the possible benefits or problems associated with each solution.

- **During daily conversations.** Students often ask their teachers or other staff members for explanations or advice. Rationales help students understand the logic behind the explanations or advice.

Final Thoughts

Although you hope students will understand your rationales and find them meaningful, the goal of using rationales is not to get students to blindly follow you or automatically agree with your reasons. Helping them understand your reasoning and modify their behavior is more important than having them agree with your point of view. Realize, too, that rationales alone often cannot effectively change behavior. They're most effective when coupled with other classroom strategies, such as establishing classroom rules, teaching social skills, and using effective consequences. In the next section, we look at how you can use those preventive strategies to set your students up for success.

Increasing Opportunities for Student Success

A POSITIVE SCHOOL CULTURE DEPENDS ON SEVERAL factors, including having staff members who are willing to model appropriate expectations, build relationships with students and their families, and act in ways that are consistent and coherent (Noonan, 2004). In the previous section, we examined the many different ways the teacher-student bond can be developed and strengthened. Now, our focus turns to the environmental factors (rules, procedures, etc.) and teaching strategies that help bring consistency to the school day and make it easier for students to find success.

According to Sugai et al. (2002), "The goal of proactive classroom management is to increase predictability and to accommodate the individual and collective needs of students" (p. 324). Increasing "predictability" in your learning community and addressing "student needs" are the primary issues examined in Section II. We begin in Chapter 6 by looking at how to create realistic and enforceable rules as a means to eliminate or reduce the chaos that can go on in classrooms and common areas. In Chapter 7, we add on procedures. Like good rules, procedures build more structure into the school day by guiding student behavior in more positive directions.

With rules and procedures, you are defining behavioral expectations for students. The next step is to empower students with the skills necessary to meet those expectations. Chapter 8 looks at how positive and negative consequences can motivate students to either change or maintain their behaviors. Sometimes, however, consequences are not enough. Many students simply lack the social skills needed to follow procedures or obey rules. In Chapter 9, we identify 16 social skills that students need to possess if they are going to contribute to a positive learning environment. Chapter 10 outlines multitiered systems of support that can help you effectively meet your students' behavioral needs. And in Chapter 11, we give you several instructional strategies for teaching necessary skills to your students.

Clarifying and Using Classroom and School Rules

A critical step in being proactive and increasing opportunities for student success is structuring your classroom to promote the behaviors you want to see. One essential component to having a structured environment is setting and using classroom and school rules.

Rules help communicate expectations. They also help create a predictable, stable environment that is more conducive to healthy, positive interactions. Ideally, rules are simple and declarative. They cannot, nor should they try to, address every conceivable problem that might arise. A laundry list of rules is hard for kids to remember, and even harder for them to follow. Instead, the most effective rules describe general expectations for behavior. Here are a few examples:

- Keep hands, feet, and objects to yourself.
  (APPROPRIATE AT THE ELEMENTARY LEVEL)

- Respect peers, teachers, and property.
  (APPROPRIATE FOR SOME MIDDLE SCHOOL STUDENTS AND
  AT THE HIGH SCHOOL LEVEL)

- Stay on task.

- Raise your hand to participate or get help.

The best classroom rules typically meet nine criteria, which we've adapted from Evertson and Emmer (1982):

1. **Rules should be stated behaviorally.** The age and developmental level of your students will dictate how behaviorally descriptive your rules need to be. Take for example the "Respect peers, teachers, and property" rule mentioned earlier. The word "respect," while not overtly specific in terms of behavior, is a general or global rule that implies actions that are behaviorally specific. Such a rule is appropriate in high schools or with students who are at a higher developmental level because they have some understanding of what respect is (although you may still have to teach them what it means to show respect to others or property). For most elementary students and many middle school students, using the word "respect" is too broad or vague. For these students, you would rephrase the rule to sound something like this: "Be quiet when others are talking." Stated this way, the rule still relates to the larger issue of respect, but the behavior-specific language is much easier for younger students to understand. They know what they are expected to do.

2. **Rules should be stated positively.** Stating a rule positively means you let students know what they are supposed to do, not just what they can't or shouldn't do. For example, having a rule that says, "No running in the hallway," does not communicate to students the behavior you DO want to see. You could tell a student not to run, only to watch him go skipping down the hall, waving his arms and shouting back at you, "You didn't say anything about skipping!" But if the rule is changed to say, "Walk in the hallways," the expectation becomes quite clear. Rules that communicate the replacement behavior you want from students are more meaningful.

   When rules are stated positively, you also reduce confusion and attempts at manipulation. For example, if a teacher relies on rules that say, "No swearing," "No slang," "No…," "No…," "No…," inevitably something gets left out. Adding more rules every time a new situation happens can overwhelm students and diminish the effectiveness of having rules.

Another advantage of stating rules positively is clarity. When rules are clear and specific, it's difficult to add stipulations or make exceptions. You want rules to be clear. You don't want rules like, "Use appropriate language WHEN…" or "No derogatory language UNLESS…." Take this situation for example: While monitoring a hallway during a passing period, a teacher overheard several of her students using the "N" word. Shocked and saddened, she approached the boys and told them the word was hurtful and violated the rule about not using derogatory language. The boys responded by saying their use of the word wasn't derogatory. They were all good buddies, and that's how they address one another. Relieved, the teacher responded, "Oh, that's okay then."

EXAMPLES OF CLASSROOM RULES

- Be on time and stay on task.
- Listen when others are speaking.
- Ask permission before leaving your seat.

But is it really okay? The teacher created an exception to the "No derogatory language" rule. What happens when other students start using the "N" word or similarly offensive terms? Are those words okay as long as the reasoning sounds innocent? Positively stated rules can eliminate all the exceptions students might come up with to manipulate a situation. Instead of a rule that says, "No derogatory language," a better option is one that says, "Use appropriate language." You may have to define what "appropriate" means by telling students to refrain from using curse words, slang, and derogatory names. But that will only help students understand your expectations regarding language and reinforce your goal of creating a civil, welcoming classroom and school. You want your students to know that being in school is not like being on the street. In school, they are expected to meet a different, often higher, standard of behavior.

3. **Rules should be developmentally appropriate.** Classroom rules should reflect the environment and the ability level of your students. Rules in a middle school classroom should look and sound different from those in an elementary classroom or high school. Likewise, rules in a tenth-grade classroom will look decidedly different from those found in a third-grade classroom. As discussed earlier, rules worded in

concrete language are better for younger students so they can understand what you're asking them to do. Older students may not need such specificity. They are much more likely to be able to conceptualize abstract ideas such as "respect" or "equality."

Using developmentally appropriate rules does not mean you need to create specific rules for each individual student. In some classrooms, the developmental range among youth can be significant, especially if special needs students are mainstreamed into general education classrooms. However, you won't have different rules for different students. What will be different is how you deal with each student's behavior and ability to follow the rules. You have to show flexibility in your expectations. For example, a second-grade class has a rule that says, "Keep your hands and feet to yourself." Most of the kids do a pretty good job of following the rule, but two students struggle. As the teacher, you would concentrate your teaching on helping the two struggling students learn what the rule means, reinforce them with praise whenever they behave appropriately, and re-teach an alternative behavior when they make a mistake. In another classroom, you have a student with severe ADHD. One of the classroom rules is "Stay on task." Obviously, you want all your students to follow the rule. However, you may have to adjust your expectations for the ADHD student. Maybe staying on task for several minutes at a time is the best he can manage, whereas the other students can stay on task for the duration of an assignment. You have to take into consideration the developmental skills of your students, and respond to their behavior accordingly.

4. **Rules should be consistent with your philosophy and the function of the class.** How you want your classroom to run reflects your philosophy. If you believe in having an open classroom where students can contribute whenever they want, you won't have a rule that says students must raise their hands, wait to be called on, and then speak. That rule doesn't jibe with a philosophy that encourages open, free discussions. You might, however, have a rule that says students should wait until a person is finished speaking before they verbalize their opinions. If your philosophy is the exact

opposite of open and unstructured, then you don't want students calling out because it would be too disruptive or inefficient. You would want a rule that says, "Raise your hand before speaking," because that conveys the philosophy of how you want your students to act in the classroom.

With regard to the function of the class, rules should reflect the environment. If you have a rule that says, "Arrive on time and be prepared," that rule will look different in different classrooms. If you're teaching music, the rule might mean students need to be in the choir room, standing in place with the appropriate song sheet. In band class, the rule might mean being in the band hall preparing the instruments. "On time" in a computer class may mean students need to be at a computer and logged in. In a physical education class, "on time" might mean being in the locker room getting dressed out.

5. **Rules should be within the parameters of the school/ district policies.** Consistency is important. You don't want to send mixed messages to students. If a school rule states that all food and beverages must remain in the cafeteria area, you shouldn't allow or say it's okay for students to bring candy or pop into your classroom. Classroom rules shouldn't undermine or contradict the rules of the school.

6. **Rules should be limited to three to five general behaviors.** Again, you don't want to have a whole laundry list of rules. Students won't be able to remember all the rules and the likelihood that they'll follow all of them decreases when there are too many. Usually, you will be able to cover the big issues or problems with three to five global rules. Go back to the "Respect peers, teachers, and property" rule discussed earlier. That broad rule encompasses many different behaviors, including fighting, vandalism, talking back, etc. Even the "Keep your hands and feet to yourself" rule, which is more behaviorally specific, is still broad enough to cover situations like these: he's touching me; she tripped me in the hallway; he's pulling my hair; she slapped me; she keeps hugging me, etc.

7. **Rules should be prominently posted.** Every classroom should have its rules posted somewhere. Display the rules on

posters that you or your students make. School rules should be posted in hallways, common areas, and classrooms. Regardless of grade level, it's nice to post rules so students have a visual reminder of the behavioral expectations and values of the school.

8. **Rules should be manageable and enforceable**. Any rule you establish should be one that you can follow up on. For example, the rule "Arrive on time and be prepared," is fairly easy to manage. You can see when your students arrive and whether they have their materials with them. If there's a school-wide rule about being on time to class because tardiness is a big problem, someone at the school should be responsible for monitoring hallways and walking through the building(s) to make sure no one is hanging out after the bell rings.

9. **Rules should be discussed and reviewed with students as needed.** At the start of a new academic year, most teachers are pretty good about reviewing rules, keeping students informed, and making sure the rules get posted. As the year progresses, unfortunately, rules tend to be forgotten until problems arise. Rather than being reactive, be proactive. Discuss and review your rules frequently.

We use the term "as needed" because there are many situations when a review of the rules makes sense: When all your students struggle with a rule; before or after an extended school break (holidays, spring, summer, etc.); prior to academic testing (for example, you might review appropriate hallway behavior because you know some students will be transitioning from room to room while others are testing); or whenever behaviors tend to spike (before special events, such as prom and homecoming). Even if your class rules are working and behavior problems are minimal, it won't hurt to remind students about the rules. This is especially true for school-wide rules. Some kids are really good about managing their behaviors and doing what needs to be done in the classroom, but when they're in less-structured settings (cafeterias, restrooms, hallways), they will act out and test the limits of what's appropriate or acceptable.

Additional Considerations

As you generate classroom rules, it's a good idea to involve the people who are most affected by them – your students. While you may not necessarily want them to write the rules, you should at least bring them into the discussion. Ask them if there's a problem or issue they want addressed. Ask them what they think a rule, such as showing respect to adults and peers, means. The more ownership students feel they have in the classroom, the less likely they will be to disregard its rules.

Rules also need to be fluid, not static. If problems arise or behaviors improve, the rules should reflect the changing environment. If your students always raise their hands before speaking in class, then that rule could be replaced with one that deals with a problem behavior that wasn't anticipated. Classroom rules should also be evaluated for their effectiveness. Are they working? Are they clear enough? Should there be more? Should there be less? If rules are going to make a difference in your classroom, they can't be forgotten. Look at the rules you have in place and make adjustments whenever necessary.

Finally, make sure others – substitutes, visitors, administrators, and parents – know what your classroom rules are. If someone visits your room and doesn't see or notice that you have posted your classroom rules, then it's likely the rules are getting lost in the classroom clutter. It's also possible your students aren't noticing them either, which defeats the whole purpose behind giving your students a visual reminder of the behavioral expectations.

EXAMPLES OF SCHOOL-WIDE RULES

- We will be responsible for our actions.
- We will include everyone in our group activities.
- We will help others if they are being bullied.

School rules can target specific problems that arise at school. Examples include bullying, tardiness, noise, cleanliness, or other issues relevant to your learning community.

School Rules

The nine criteria that help make classroom rules successful should also be applied when formulating school-wide rules. Unlike classroom rules, school rules require involvement from administrators and staff. To develop consistency in the building and ensure that everyone is reading from the same book, school rules should be crafted during staff meetings or in-service days prior to the start of the school year. Getting staff input helps build consensus and makes it more likely the rules will target the most problematic or pressing issues.

Some school officials are reluctant to spend time creating school-wide rules because they already have a handbook that describes in detail all of their rules and policies. Handbooks are good, but how often are they actually read? A handbook doesn't give staff or students that daily reminder of what behavior is expected during the school day. That's why we recommend picking three to five rules out of the handbook to emphasize during the year, or writing new rules that address issues or problems that staff see as reoccurring. Whatever rules you decide to emphasize should be posted prominently throughout the building.

Here are a few examples of school-wide rules:

- Follow the directions of all staff.

- Be respectful of school property.

- Use appropriate language.

Final Thoughts

Rules are the first layer in a preventive strategy to bring structure to a classroom and school. But to have a healthy, well-functioning learning environment requires more effort than just making up rules. In the next chapter, we look at how you can use procedures to help students follow the rules you have in place. Procedures, whether they describe how to go to the cafeteria or how to hand in assignments, can diminish much of the chaos that goes on during a typical school day.

Establishing and Teaching Classroom and School Procedures

In the previous chapter, we described how classroom and school rules can convey behavior expectations to students. Now we look at how you can make those rules easier for students to understand and follow by setting up procedures. Procedures support your rules and establish routines for safe and orderly transitions. When rules are coupled with procedures, students have specific directions on how to accomplish tasks and manage their behaviors.

Ideally, procedures bring structure and control to situations that can be confusing or chaotic. On a typical school day, there are many moments when having established procedures can minimize disruptions and distractions. Some of these situations can include when students are turning in assignments, working at activity centers, and transitioning from one project or classroom to another. Here is an example that illustrates how having a procedure can help restore order to a situation that is out of hand:

> Ms. Jackson-Jones taught seventh-grade geography. But looking into her classroom, you might mistake it for an art studio. She had her students drawing maps, charting mountain ranges, tracing great rivers, and sketching large landmasses. Students used color pencils in their diagrams to distinguish farmlands from forests and seas from deserts, so the room's lone pencil sharpener was in near-constant use. Unfortunately, sharpening the point of a pencil wasn't all that students did. Other behaviors included shoving, stabbing,

gossiping, grabbing, yelling, and laughing. All manner of disruptive, sometimes even dangerous, behaviors went on whenever students gathered around the pencil sharpener. And whatever horseplay happened there continued when students returned to their desks or work groups. Sometimes the behavior would get so unruly, Ms. Jackson-Jones had to end the in-class activities and return to lecturing about the subject matter. That was a quick fix, but not a long-term solution, especially since many of her students were visual learners. Even though there were classroom rules about respect and consequences for acting out (using consequences effectively is described in Chapter 8), the students could never seem to maintain appropriate behavior when two or more of them stood at the pencil sharpener.

Because the students demonstrated a lack of maturity and responsibility, Ms. Jackson-Jones knew they needed more supervision. So she developed a procedure that restricted their use of the pencil sharpener and helped them better manage their behaviors. If a student wanted to sharpen a pencil, he or she had to ask permission first. And only one student at a time was allowed at the sharpener. This eliminated situations where students could get up and wander around the room, especially when they saw their friends sharpening pencils. If the teacher gave permission, the student had to walk quietly to the sharpener, quickly sharpen the pencil(s), and quietly walk back to his or her desk or workstation. This also dramatically reduced the noise level in the room. By setting up this procedure, Ms. Jackson-Jones was able to effectively eliminate one of the biggest sources of disruption in her classroom.

This classroom situation exemplifies how evaluating your environment, identifying the antecedents of inappropriate behavior, and then altering those antecedents (in this case, putting limits on the use of the pencil sharpener) can positively and dramatically affect changes in behavior. Establishing sound procedures is a critical component in any attempt to create a structured, more harmonious learning environment. Or as Harry and Rosemary Wong (2004) succinctly state in their popular book *The First Days of School*, "Every classroom needs to have a set of procedures. Procedures allow the class to operate smoothly. A smooth-running, effective classroom is free of confusion and is a pleasure to teach and learn in" (p. 171).

Guidelines for Developing Procedures

Procedures, whether they're for sharpening pencils or dining in the cafeteria, encourage positive and productive actions from students by giving them specific directions on what they need to do. The more specific the directions, the easier it should be to get things done in your classroom.

Procedures support and are similar to rules in that both need to meet certain criteria to be effective. When setting up procedures in a classroom or school, it's useful to follow these guidelines, which we've adapted from Evertson and Emmer (1982):

1. **Decide what you want to accomplish in your classroom.** What is your ultimate goal for how you want your classroom to look and work? The best way to think about this is to visualize in your mind a perfectly running classroom. What has to be done, procedurally, to make your vision a reality so your classroom runs as smoothly as possible? It may be helpful to think about potential problems. Are there activities or situations that have the potential to cause chaos or disruptions?

   From the perspective of the school, think about what needs to be done so the school day runs smoothly. What can be done to foster a positive, warm environment for students? Are there areas of the building or certain periods during the day where students need more structure and direction? If there are multiple problem areas, which ones can or should be addressed immediately? Procedurally, what can be done to help students? What can be done to strengthen and support the rules in the classroom and the school? (It can be helpful to create a school team – administrators, teachers, and support staff – whose role is to answer these questions and then develop standard procedures for common areas such as hallways and cafeterias.)

   When you're looking at the entire school environment, multiple problem areas may exist that require change. However, addressing each one simultaneously may prove difficult. We recommend addressing the most pressing problem first. We consider the most pressing problem to be the one that causes the most disruption, affects the most individuals, and has the potential, if corrected, to bring about the greatest positive change in the overall school climate.

2. **Determine what behaviors your students need to use.** Once you have an image of your ideal classroom and school, think about the skills and behaviors your students need to demonstrate in order to make that vision a reality. For example, one teacher visualizes a classroom where some students work on an assignment at their desks, others gather around his desk for extra help, and the remaining students, who finish their assignments early, work independently at one of the activity centers in the room. In this teacher's vision, all of the students stay on task, allowing him to provide one-on-one attention to those who need extra help. To make his vision a reality, students need to know how to turn in their assignments and what to do while others are still working or asking for help.

3. **Identify the steps of the procedures students are expected to follow that will support a positive learning climate.** The fewer and more simplified the steps (three or fewer is best), the easier it is for students to follow a procedure. And when students can understand and follow a procedure, the easier it becomes to manage their behaviors.

Using the previous example, the teacher has to specify the actions he wants his students to take when they turn in their assignments and when they are waiting for others to finish. The procedure he creates might include these instructions:

- When you finish your assignment, walk to the front of the room, place your assignment sheet in the class folder, and return to your seat.

- Then, take out a book to read, work on an assignment from another class, or go to an activity center and do independent work.

When breaking down a procedure into its behavioral steps, you don't want to give students the option of doing nothing. Kids should always have something constructive to do. This is especially important when you have to turn your attention away from the class to take care of something unexpected – an administrator needs to talk to you, a parent comes to the door, a student becomes ill and needs you to escort him to the nurse's office, a new student needs to be enrolled in the class, or a student acts out and you have to focus on de-escalating her behavior.

At Boys Town schools, we have a procedure for such interruptions. We use "DEAR Time," which stands for "Drop Everything And Read." In a situation where you cannot continue your lesson plan and the students cannot go on without you, a procedure like DEAR Time (or Independent Time) helps students manage their behaviors and controls the situation. Procedurally, DEAR Time looks something like this:

- Drop everything (stop what you're doing).

- Take out reading material (text book, novel, magazine).

- Read quietly until you're given further instructions.

Hopefully, such disruptions are rare in your classroom. But they can happen, and they have the potential to trigger disruptive and unruly behavior from students when there is no direction or plan in place.

4. **Post procedures (if you deem it necessary).** Visual reminders of certain procedures can be reinforcing and serve as learning aides, especially for students who are struggling and need additional prompts or are visual learners. However, it probably isn't necessary to post the steps of every procedure, especially when students demonstrate they have certain ones mastered. If you're unsure whether posting the steps of a procedure is worthwhile, we recommend erring on the side of giving students more prompts or reminders. This is especially true if you are implementing a new procedure in response to a problem, as was the case in Ms. Jackson-Jones' geography class. Her students needed to see the new procedures for using the pencil sharpener spelled

out because it was such a departure from what they were used to and because the sharpener was the site and cause of so much chaos.

You also want to avoid the trap of saying to a student, "I've talked about this once already. You should know what to do." One discussion is usually not enough, and making such an assumption only sets you and the student up for failure. Most likely, there are going to be some procedures that students will need to be repeatedly reminded about, either verbally or visually. Finally, it's a good idea to include the explanations or steps of your classroom or school procedures in a file that can be accessed by substitute teachers and volunteers.

5. **Teach and review these procedures as needed.** At the start of a new academic year, students should see and hear frequent reminders about behavior expectations BEFORE, not after, they get into trouble. As the year progresses, continue to review the procedures, especially before or after extended school breaks, or whenever you have situations that are chaotic and confusing. Evaluate your procedures based on the vision you have of a perfectly managed and well-run classroom or school. Decide what, if anything, is preventing that vision from becoming a reality. If a procedure isn't working as nicely as you want it to, consider adding another behavioral step or changing one. Maybe you just need to explain the procedure again or change the way you teach it to your students. Perhaps an entirely different procedure is required. Also, each academic year ushers in a new group of students who have different relationships that change the dynamics of the classroom. For that reason, what worked one year may not work the next.

You also want to be watchful that students aren't manipulating any of the procedures that are in place. Take for example DEAR Time. If students know you're going to say "DEAR Time" whenever someone acts up in class, a student might intentionally escalate his or her behavior to show others he or she has the power to stop the class. Or, students may encourage someone to act up so they can have DEAR Time to finish a reading assignment that's due next period. If you suspect students are taking advantage of a procedure or manipulating its true intent, address your concerns with the class. Explain the purpose of the procedure and the potential consequences for anyone who tries to abuse or manipulate its use.

Equally important, however, is recognizing and praising students when they follow procedures. A positive statement, such as, "Class, nice job using DEAR Time. When you follow instructions and sit quietly, I can help others more quickly," is a nice way of acknowledging their efforts. You might also consider more concrete rewards to reinforce their positive behavior. Depending on their age or skill level, you could reward them with an extended recess or additional minutes on the computer, or allow them to skip a problem on their homework sheet.

Final Thoughts

The real value of procedures is the specificity and guidance they provide for an individual's behavior. Any procedures you develop should reflect the skill level and age of your students. When procedures are combined with rules, you have a foundation for shaping behaviors in a positive direction. In other words, you are setting your students up to be successful. Here are more examples of how procedures can bring order to situations where disorder is common:

Using the Restroom
Only three students may be in the restroom at a time.
There is a three-minute time limit.
Keep hands, feet, and objects to yourself.
Wash your hands before you leave.

Going to an Assembly
Walk quietly in the hallway.
Sit in your assigned area.
Listen attentively.
Clap at the appropriate time, in an appropriate manner.
Wait to be dismissed.

Eating in the Cafeteria
Wait in line calmly.
Use a pleasant voice to request the food you want.

Say "Thank you" to cafeteria staff.
Walk to your table.
Eat and talk using low voices.
Clean up your area and return the food tray.

Coming Prepared to Class
Have all your materials with you when entering class.*
Go directly to your seat.
Get your materials out and put them on your desk.
Sit quietly while the teacher gives instructions.

* May not be applicable in an elementary setting.

8

Understanding and Giving Consequences

Establishing classroom and school-wide rules and procedures are important steps in any effort to bring more structure and order to your learning environment. Still, no matter how clearly these expectations are stated to students, don't expect complete compliance. Rules and procedures by themselves do not motivate students to change behavior. In fact, many students will push the limits and violate expectations to test how much they can get away with. Students also like to test their teachers' tolerance levels and find out whether or not their teachers will back up their words with actions. That's why consequences are so important. Much of what motivates students to follow rules and procedures and meet behavioral expectations comes from consequences – the benefits they earn for complying with or exceeding expectations and the disadvantages they earn by violating established standards.

Wong and Wong (2004) encourage educators to equate consequences with choices. Every action has a reaction or result, and consequences are the results of personal choices by the student – not you or someone else. Sometimes, students like to deflect blame onto other people or circumstances. Effective consequences show young people the connection between what they do and what happens as a result of their choices or actions.

In Chapter 3, we introduced the ABC's of behavior (the three-term contingency pattern). The "A" stands for antecedent or antecedent event. This is the situation or condition that exists before a student's behavior or performance of a skill. The "B" is the behavior – whatever a student says or does that can be directly or indirectly observed. And the "C" represents the consequence – the reaction or response (positive or negative) to an action. In this chapter, we examine what consequences look like and why some are more effective than others.

Effective Consequences

Oftentimes, educators feel that no matter what they try, the consequences they give are not effective. It's important to remember that change takes time. A consequence may not change a behavior the first time it is used. You need to be patient and look for small improvements, giving the consequence time to work. The best consequences not only motivate students, but also teach them that appropriate behaviors (following instructions, disagreeing appropriately, accepting criticism, etc.) represent the most efficient and effective means for attaining their goals. There are certain conditions or factors that influence whether or not consequences will produce the desired behavior from students. They include:

- **Appropriateness.** Consequences need to be individualized to students so they are meaningful. For example, if a student loses a recess as a negative consequence for not completing an assignment, the consequence won't be motivating if the student hates recess. (It may actually reinforce the negative behavior because the student avoids something he or she doesn't enjoy.) Consequences, whether positive or negative, have to hold some value to the student; otherwise, he or she will not be motivated to change an inappropriate behavior or maintain an appropriate one.

- **Immediacy.** To maximize their effectiveness, consequences need to be used immediately after the behavior. The more time that passes between the occurrence of the behavior and the consequence, the less effective the consequence may be. For example, giving immediate verbal praise after a student correctly answers a question is more likely to make the student want to participate in the class and learn the material being taught.

- **Size.** The size of the consequence should mirror the behavior. The size of a reward can be based on such criteria as how long the behavior takes to perform, if it's a new behavior or skill for a student, and how difficult it is. A negative consequence can be measured in terms of the frequency, severity, or duration of the misbehavior. A sense of proportion must be exercised when using consequences. If they're too punishing, students may give up and lose hope. If they're too trivial, students may decide it's not worth the effort.

- **Consistency.** If you address a certain behavior on Monday, you shouldn't ignore that same behavior on Friday. When consequences are unpredictable and inconsistent, there's little incentive for students to follow rules or continue to engage in an appropriate behavior. Being consistent also means demonstrating fairness. The ADHD child should be praised for his or her efforts and good behavior as much as the athletically or academically gifted child. Similarly, consequences for inappropriate behaviors should not be based on the relationship you have with a student (e.g. giving an "easy" consequence to a student you like or giving a "difficult" consequence to a student you don't like). All students need to be held accountable; how that looks should be individualized according to the student's needs, history, or ability.

- **Consequence contingencies.** A student must receive a consequence only AFTER performing the behavior. Rewarding students for behaviors that didn't happen or punishing students without cause is as damaging as never using consequences at all.

  A contingency is an "If... then" statement: If a person does a behavior, he or she gets the consequence. For example, "If you finish questions one through five at the end of the chapter, then you may talk quietly with your neighbors," or "If you remain in your seat until I finish the lecture, then you may go to the shelf and get your journal." Positive consequences need to be contingent on positive behavior. You also must analyze negative behavior to determine whether you might be giving consequences that are inadvertently reinforcing or strengthening that negative behavior.

- **Consequence satiation and deprivation.** A positive consequence is more meaningful when an individual doesn't have constant access to it. Overuse or overexposure to the same positive consequence can lead to satiation. Satiation occurs when a child has had so much of the same positive consequence that it no longer works as a positive reinforcer. For example, if a child who has been working on the computer for 20 minutes displays a positive behavior, having the child earn more computer time as a positive consequence might not be effective because it is no longer meaningful to the child. Using a variety of reinforcers and using ones that are most in demand by students at the moment maximizes the effectiveness of positive consequences.

The opposite of satiation is deprivation. Deprivation occurs when an individual does not have repeated access to, or enough of, a positive reinforcer. While satiation can potentially decrease the effectiveness of a reinforcer, deprivation potentially increases its effectiveness.

Negative consequences also can lose their effectiveness if they are overused. If losing recess time or computer time is the only consequence a student earns for negative behavior, that consequence eventually becomes ineffective because the student will learn to live without recess or adjust to limited computer time.

When giving a consequence, it's important for students to understand that their behavior earned the consequence and that they have to take ownership of their actions. This is especially important when students are being corrected for misbehaviors. You can reinforce the idea of personal responsibility to students by clearly stating that the consequence is a result of something they did. For example, you should avoid statements such as, "I'm taking away…" or "I'm never letting you…." A better approach is to say something like, "Because you interrupted Jacinda's presentation with your snickering and loud sighs, you're going to have to stay after class instead of going to the assembly." This reinforces the fact that the student's behavior caused the negative consequence.

Here are some key points for delivering consequences:

Be specific. Make sure students know what the consequence is and exactly what they did to earn it.

Be consistent. Don't give a big consequence for a behavior one time and then ignore the behavior the next time it occurs.

Be brief. Clear messages about behavior can get lost if you lecture endlessly.

Follow through. If you tell a student he or she earned a negative or positive consequence, follow through with it. If a student talks you out of a negative consequence or you fail to provide a promised reinforcer, the student's incentive to change or maintain behavior is lost.

Be as pleasant as possible. Verbal praise that sounds insincere or unenthusiastic loses its intent. Likewise, remaining calm and reasonable when explaining a negative consequence can keep students from escalating their behaviors.

Consequence Overload?

There can be times when students earn too many consequences. This tends to happen more with negative behaviors than positive ones. That's because we have a tendency to notice mistakes more than successes. This is unfortunate because research indicates that positive behavior management strategies are more successful than punishing, reactive responses (Mayer, 1999).

In our experience, most schools are not overloading their students with positive praise. But how do you decide if a consequence is necessary? Does every appropriate action require reinforcement, and does each minor misbehavior deserve a response?

Knowing when to give consequences relates somewhat to how well you know your students. When you're teaching new behaviors or social skills, constant reinforcement is essential. Likewise, when there's a behavior problem that is frequent or severe, it cannot be ignored. Fortunately, there are many instances when a quick comment or subtle gesture can communicate approval or prompt students to get back on task. We'll talk more about those strategies in Chapters 12 and 13. Right now, let's review two basic schedules of reinforcement – continuous and intermittent – you can follow when delivering positive consequences.

A **continuous schedule** means a consequence is given every time a student or group of students displays a specific, targeted behavior. A continuous schedule of reinforcement is best whenever you're teaching a new behavior or skill to students. You want to encourage and strengthen their continued use of the skill, so students should earn rewards frequently whenever they demonstrate that behavior.

Once the behavior or skill becomes part of the student's routine and he or she repeatedly demonstrates or uses it appropriately and in appropriate situations, the reinforcement can move to an intermittent schedule. On an **intermittent schedule**, targeted behaviors and skills are reinforced periodically. For example, you can give a positive consequence every other time or every third time the behavior is performed, or on any schedule based on frequency or time. This may seem a bit counterintuitive, but intermittent schedules of reinforcement actually strengthen a behavior or skill better than continuous reinforcement. The element of surprise and not knowing when the reinforcement is coming keeps the student's use of a behavior or skill occurring on a more consistent basis. Intermittent schedules also help fade consequences to a more reality-based schedule. In life, as you know, positive rewards do not follow every instance of doing something well. Students can learn this lesson through fading. Your ultimate goal is to help students internalize positive rewards through feelings of self-satisfaction.

Examples of Positive Consequences

The consequences you can use to acknowledge and reinforce positive student behavior are almost limitless. They can be big and obvious or small and subtle. Most positive rewards can be grouped into three distinct types – tangibles, activities, and socials.

Tangible consequences are objects or possessions students can earn after demonstrating a positive behavior. They can include special stickers, treats, toys, special passes or exemptions, and positive notes home to parents.

Activity-oriented consequences are events or privileges. Passing out papers, choosing a lab partner, or earning extra time on the computer are rewards that reflect an activity that a student enjoys. An added benefit is that many activities do not have a direct cost. They are a popular alternative to tangible consequences, which require greater financial flexibility.

Social consequences are rewards that should occur daily in classrooms and schools. Physical contact (high-fives and pats on the back), proximity (standing or sitting near an individual), and verbal praise ("Good job," "Awesome effort," etc.) are all powerful examples of social encouragement and reinforcement. (Proximity can also be used to stop negative behaviors, like moving toward or standing closer to students who are talking when they should be silent.)

In Chapter 12, we'll examine the value of praise statements. Chapters 13 and 14 describe how positive and negative consequences can be a natural byproduct of teaching interactions.

Potentially Harmful Consequences

Negative consequences also can take many forms, but they typically involve actions such as verbal reprimands, phone calls or notes home to parents, unwanted attention from a teacher or administrator, after-school detentions, in-school suspensions, expulsions, and corporal punishment. (Boys Town considers corporal punishment an ineffective, inappropriate, and unnecessary response. Such actions only serve to model aggression to students, many of whom desperately need to learn healthier coping skills and prosocial behaviors. Suppressing behavior through coercive means has only a temporary effect; aversive discipline methods too often result in counter-aggression, and even violence, from students.)

Unfortunately, the frustrations felt by some adults during emotionally intense situations or moments of stress can lead to reactions or circumstances where students are victimized. Sometimes, negative consequences are used inappropriately and actually threaten a child's physical and emotional well-being. In our work with school systems across the country, we've seen some harsh and punitive punishments that are more hurtful than helpful, including:

- **Isolation and removal.** In some classrooms, students who present the greatest behavior challenges are frequently sent out of the classroom. Sometimes, their behavior simply overwhelmed the teacher. Other times, however, removing the student from the classroom, and even the school, appeared to be an attempt to solve a problem with the least amount of effort and energy (not to mention potentially giving a boost to test scores used to measure whether academic achievement standards are being met). It's important to note, however, that legislation like the Individuals with Disability Act and the Safe and Drug Free Communities of No Child Left Behind demands that educators show proof of using some type of preventive intervention strategy before they suspend or expel students who are emotionally or behaviorally disabled. Whenever a student is temporarily isolated or removed from a classroom, the incident should be recorded.

- **Denial of nourishment.** We've seen instances where students were denied lunch as punishment for their inappropriate behavior. Ironically, students who are hungry have difficulty concentrating on their academic work, and oftentimes, their hunger fuels more irritability. Food and water cannot be denied. Instead, other reasonable limitations can be applied. For example, a student may be restricted to a certain area during lunch (sitting at an assigned table or eating in another area outside of the cafeteria and away from classmates). Other limitations, such as setting specific times for students to obtain drinks, are acceptable.

- **Loss of personal possessions.** Students do not waive the right to privacy when they bring personal possessions on to school grounds. However, educators can exercise reasonable control over what students are allowed to bring onto school grounds and into individual classrooms. Obviously, dangerous items (weapons, drugs, etc.) should be confiscated and turned over to law enforcement. Other potentially disruptive items, including cell phones, can be restricted and their use limited. Outlining these restrictions in the student handbook is helpful. However, taking away essential supplies that students need to perform their work is unacceptable.

Other forms of punishment that sometimes are taken to extremes, thus becoming more about humiliation and revenge than behavioral support and teaching, include corporal punishment, demeaning verbal reprimands or labels (idiot, thug, gang banger, loser, etc.), and extended periods of time-out or exclusion. When these consequences define the discipline practices of any school, achieving a positive social climate is almost impossible. Worse, the instructional and academic needs of students are damaged.

Final Thoughts

Positive consequences are critical to students' success and building a sense of community. They should be valued as much and used as often as any traditional form of discipline. We talk a lot about creating "community' in school. The effective use of consequences can have a profound effect on whether or not students feel connected to their learning environment. When a student does something inappropriate – like acting out in a classroom, for example – that disrupts other members of the community, that student has violated a bond of trust between students in the community. If students learn to see themselves as socially responsible members of the school community, they will not want to disappoint other members of that community by acting in ways that are disruptive or harmful.

Together, negative and positive consequences represent one element in a comprehensive behavior management plan. In the next two chapters, you will learn how social skills instruction can empower young people to get their needs met without violating the needs of others.

The Value of Social and Emotional Learning, and Social Skills

For many young people, school is the biggest challenge in their lives. The stress of trying to achieve academic success is often compounded by other worries related to school life – having friends, making the team, getting along with classmates and teachers, being bullied, getting teased, having boyfriends or girlfriends, etc. As much as we want students to try their best and earn good grades, many would gladly give up an "A" in exchange for fitting in and being accepted. That's how much relationships matter.

Children who struggle with their relationships at school often lack basic social skills. In other words, they don't know what to do or how to respond or behave in certain social situations. These social deficiencies, if not improved or corrected, can haunt children long after they leave the classroom. There is evidence that social and behavioral deficiencies that are ignored in childhood frequently carry over into adulthood (Steinberg & Knitzer, 1992). Meadows, Neel, Parker, and Timo (1991) found that adults who had social skill deficits as children suffered long-term effects ranging from higher rates of suicide to unsuccessful employment histories. The link between poor social skills and other problems is clear. In the classroom, young people who lack social skills can suffer from a variety of problems, including aggressive and antisocial behavior, juvenile delinquency, learning problems, mental health disorders, loneliness, despondency, and school failure (Coie & Jacobs, 1993; Walker et al., 2004).

Social and Emotional Learning

To help educators resolve (or at least minimize) the difficult and challenging behaviors they face in the classroom, experts in whole-child education and child development have advocated that more attention and focus be given to the social and emotional competencies of children.

Social and emotional learning (SEL) is defined by the Collaborative for Academic, Social, and Emotional Learning (CASEL) as the process "through which children and adults acquire and effectively apply the knowledge, attitudes, and skills necessary to understand and manage emotions, set and achieve positive goals, feel and show empathy for others, establish and maintain positive relationships, and make responsible decisions" (CASEL, 2012, p.4).

SEL is fundamental to character development, and is important to children's "health, ethical development, citizenship, academic learning, and motivation to achieve" (Elias, Parker, Kash, Weissberg, & O'Brien, 2008, p. 253). In fact, research is expanding beyond this to measure the positive effects of the systematic implementation of social and emotional development strategies.

Evidence suggests that disruptive student behaviors negatively affect the academic learning of all members of a class. Not only is academic learning affected, but the lack of social and emotional competence by youth in schools contributes to harmful and risky behaviors, hopelessness, and a lack of safety.

For example, recent data from the Centers for Disease Control and Prevention found the following (Kann et al., 2014):

- Nationally, 7.1 percent of students in grades 9 through 12 were truant or did not attend school on one or more of the previous 30 days prior to the survey because they felt unsafe at school, on their way to school, or on their way home from school.

- Nationally, 6.9 percent of students reported being threatened with or harmed by a weapon, such as a gun or knife, on school property at least once in the 12 months prior to the survey.

- Consistent feelings of sadness or hopelessness afflicted 29.9 percent of students. They reported having those feelings almost every day for two weeks or more in a row during the previous 12 months – so much so that they stopped doing some of their usual activities.

- Most alarmingly, 13.6 percent reported not only suicide ideation, but also actually having a plan to attempt suicide during this period.

This data supports the need for ongoing development of children's social and emotional competence.

The following pages describe the five competencies for social and emotional learning as defined by CASEL (2012, 2013).

Five Competencies for Social and Emotional Learning

Self-Awareness: The ability to…

- Recognize and label own emotions.
- Identify what triggers those emotions.
- Analyze emotions and how they affect others.
- Accurately recognize own strengths and limitations.
- Identify own needs and values.
- Possess self-efficacy and self-esteem.

Youth who are more self-aware tend to exhibit self-confidence and a hopeful sense of the future.

Self-Management: The ability to…

- Set plans and work toward goals.
- Overcome obstacles.
- Manage stress.
- Seek help.
- Regulate impulses and emotions.
- Maintain attention.
- Exhibit motivation and hope.
- Persevere.

The ability to manage oneself and regulate impulses leads to fewer risky behaviors and greater achievement of goals.

Social Awareness: The ability to…

- Identify social cues (a particular challenge for students with Autism Spectrum Disorder).
- Predict others' feelings and reactions.
- Evaluate others' reactions.
- Show respect for others.
- Understand other points of view or perspectives.
- Appreciate diversity.
- Identify and use resources in one's family, school, and community.

The ability to exhibit empathy and identify and rely on available resources in the environment (family, school, and community) increases the likelihood that a child will develop positive relationships.

Relationship Skills: The ability to…

- Make friends.
- Learn cooperatively and work toward group goals.
- Communicate with others.
- Provide help to those who need it.
- Manage and express emotions in relationships while respecting diverse viewpoints.
- Resist inappropriate social pressures.

Responsible Decision-Making: The ability to…

- Reflect on how current choices affect the future.
- Make decisions based on moral, personal, and ethical standards.
- Identify problems when making decisions and generate alternative options.
- Negotiate fairly.
- Become self-reflective and self-evaluative.

Ultimately, it is the goal of most parents, educators, and youth-serving professionals to ensure the children in their care are able to develop positive, responsible decision-making skills.

If you are going to help students achieve success in the classroom and the community, focusing on social and emotional learning and social skills instruction is a necessity. Historically, many educators have been reluctant to incorporate the purposeful teaching of social skills into their school day. Instead, it was often a "hidden curriculum" in which certain rules and behavioral guidelines were used and enforced to make group teaching more manageable. But beyond that, little attention was paid to empowering students to make better decisions.

According to Goleman (2005), there are many other ways to measure success and intelligence than by simply using traditional academic testing. Goleman's work outlined a multi-faceted approach to measuring competence in critical domains of life and in measuring success in school beyond academics. Developing competencies in each of these social and emotional domains gives an individual a better opportunity to attain lifelong success in a variety of areas.

Skill Types and Executive Function

In addition to the importance of developing social and emotional competence, recent research on the development of the whole child has identified a set of essential life skills. These skills, which center on a child's ability to plan, organize, and manage complex tasks, impact a child's ability to achieve in school, to prepare and be ready for the future workforce, and to avoid a host of other problems. While children aren't born with these skills, they are born with the capacity to develop them. These skills develop throughout childhood, into the teen years, and even into early adulthood. The quality of children's interactions with adults, peers, and the community greatly influences whether these skills are developed fully, or are diminished (Center on the Developing Child at Harvard University, 2011).

These cognitive processes are commonly known as "executive function." Incorporation of the term "executive" in referencing these skills is attributed to Karl Pribram (1973, 1976). A deficit in these skills is labeled as "executive dysfunction" or "executive function deficit." These deficits are considered to have neurocognitive as well as behavioral symptoms (Baddeley, 1986; Wilson, Evans, Alderman, Burgess, & Emslie, 1997; Barkley, 2012). Examples of executive functions include impulse control, emotional control, flexibility, working memory, self-monitoring, planning and prioritizing, task initiation, and organization (Morin, 2014).

Here are the categories and descriptions of skill types that cross multiple executive function processes.

Social Skills

Skills in this category are related to most situations in which a person interacts with another person or other people. These situations might range from having a private, one-on-one conversation with a friend, to asking directions from a stranger, to being with a small group of people in a doctor's waiting room, to being part of large crowd at a party. Social skills enable a person to appropriately communicate with, respond to, make a request from, and get along with other people.

Emotional Management Skills

Emotional management skills enable a person to find and maintain a balance between not feeling anything and letting one's feelings control his or her behavior. These skills also help a person maintain self-control, stay calm in exciting, stressful, or frustrating situations, and make good choices under pressure. One major area where this is important is anger control. People who know which skills to use to prevent or control their anger and not become physically or verbally aggressive are able to stay out of trouble and solve problems or overcome obstacles in appropriate ways.

Academic Skills

Completing homework and turning it in on time, studying, taking tests, reading, doing learning activities, and taking notes during lectures are just a few of the areas where having good academic skills are necessary. And while we usually associate academics only with school, these skills are useful in any learning situation, whether it is with a teacher in a classroom, reading a book, or working on a computer to expand one's knowledge.

Ethical/Moral Skills

Skills that help a person learn positive ethics and morals contribute to building character and developing a conscience. A person's ability to use ethical/moral skills provides the "moral compass" that helps him or her know right from wrong, good from bad, and prosocial from antisocial. Good character stems from knowing the right thing to do and following through.

Independent-Living Skills

People are able to perform the activities of life – cooking, shopping, keeping up an apartment or house, managing finances, balancing a checkbook, looking for a job, buying a car and making payments, and many others – because they have learned how to take care of themselves. Independent-living skills prepare people to be on their own and to contribute to society as a wage earner, a good neighbor, a productive citizen, and an independent person.

For decades, Boys Town has emphasized the development of the whole child, including building social competence, so children are empowered to be lifelong self-managers and problem-solvers. Our experience and research confirm that teaching social skills is an effective way of fostering children's social competence.

In the previous chapters, we outlined why rules and procedures are important components in any effort to shape students' behaviors. But as essential as they are, their long-term effectiveness is limited if a social skills component is not included. Social skills instruction is necessary to support your rules and procedures.

The Social Skills

Social (or life) skills are sets of behaviors that enable individuals to interact with one another in ways that are socially acceptable and personally beneficial, mutually beneficial, or beneficial to others. By teaching children social skills, we help them learn new ways of thinking, new ways of feeling good, and new ways of behaving. Social skills are not a constant set of behaviors. They vary, depending on the context or situation in which they are to be used. Using social skills in appropriate ways, across a variety of contexts, is a complex process. It involves more than knowing a set of behaviors;

rather, it means making a rapid chain of decisions based on reading cues and determining responses in the framework of interpersonal interactions. This is also called "code-switching," which is discussed in Chapter 11.

In our decades of experience working with students and educators from every conceivable geographic and socio-economic environment, we've identified 16 social skills that are the foundation of a well-managed classroom and school. Students who have and use the following skills can contribute greatly to a positive learning environment:

Following Instructions
1. Look at the person.
2. Say "Okay."
3. Do what you've been asked right away.
4. Check back (when instructed).

Accepting Criticism or a Consequence
1. Look at the person.
2. Say "Okay."
3. Stay calm.

Accepting "No" for an Answer
1. Look at the person.
2. Say "Okay."
3. Stay calm.
4. If you disagree, ask later.

Greeting Others
1. Look at the person.
2. Use a pleasant voice.
3. Say "Hi" or "Hello."

Getting the Teacher's Attention
1. Look at the teacher.
2. Raise your hand and stay calm.
3. Wait until the teacher says your name.
4. Ask your question.

Disagreeing Appropriately

1. Look at the person.
2. Use a pleasant voice.
3. Tell why you feel differently.
4. Give a reason.
5. Listen to the other person.

Making an Apology (Saying You're Sorry)

1. Look at the person.
2. Use a serious, sincere voice.
3. Say "I'm sorry for..." or "I want to apologize for...."
4. Explain how you plan to do better in the future.
5. Say "Thanks for listening."

Accepting Compliments

1. Look at the person.
2. Use a pleasant voice.
3. Say "Thank you."

Having a Conversation

1. Look at the person.
2. Use a pleasant voice.
3. Listen to what the other person says.
4. When there is a break in the conversation, ask a question or share your thoughts.

Asking for Help

1. Look at the person.
2. Ask the person if he or she has time to help you.
3. Clearly explain the kind of help you need.
4. Thank the person for helping.

Asking Permission

1. Look at the person.
2. Use a calm and pleasant voice.
3. Say "May I...?"
4. Accept the answer calmly.

Staying on Task

1. Look at your task or assignment.
2. Think about the steps needed to complete the task.

3. Focus all of your attention on the task.
4. Stop working only when instructed.
5. Ignore distractions and interruptions from others.

Sharing with Others

1. Let the other person use the item first.
2. Ask if you can use it later.
3. When you get to use it, offer it back to the other person after you're finished.

Working with Others (Being a Team)

1. Identify the task to be completed.
2. Assign tasks to each person.
3. Discuss ideas in a calm, quiet voice and let everyone share their ideas.
4. Work on tasks until completed.

Listening to Others

1. Look at the person who is talking and remain quiet.
2. Wait until the person is finished talking before you speak.
3. Show that you heard the person by nodding your head, saying "Okay" or "That's interesting," etc.

Using an Appropriate Voice Tone

1. Listen to the level of the voices around you.
2. Change your voice tone to match.
3. Watch and listen for visual or verbal cues and adjust your voice as needed.

These social skills set the foundation for creating a well-functioning classroom and school, as well as supporting your mission or values. As you can see, each of these skills is broken down into specific and observable steps. When you teach social skills to students, it's important to identify their behavioral steps. Each step should be measurable and observable so students can clearly understand what is expected of them. This also helps them have more success when they use a skill. Identifying and defining the elements of a social skill can be done through a process called "task analysis" (Cartledge & Milburn, 1978).

Task Analysis

Every social skill – not just the ones described earlier – can be broken down and taught in a step-by-step manner. You simply start by deciding what you want the student to do. That is, begin with the end goal in mind. Once you know your end product, identify what behaviors need to be included to get the desired result. Make sure each step is observable so you can tell whether the student is meeting your expectations. Include only critical steps, so the skill doesn't become so complicated no one can remember all of its components. The most effective way to task-analyze any skill is to follow these guidelines:

- Keep the focus of the skill limited.

- Identify behaviors of the skill as steps.

- Use specific and observable terms.

- Put steps in a logical order of performance.

By task-analyzing a skill, you connect the social skill (which is often an abstract concept to most students) to tangible, concrete actions that students can understand. Here is how one group of teachers task-analyzed the skill of "Introducing Yourself":

Introducing Yourself

1. **Look at the person. Smile.**
   This is a good first step because looking at someone and smiling is a way to communicate your desire to meet him or her.

2. **Use a pleasant voice.**
   This is a necessary step because a pleasant voice allows you to make a positive first impression.

3. **Offer a greeting. Say, "Hi, my name is…."**
   Saying "Hi" helps make the other person feel welcome.

4. **Shake the person's hand.**
   This step makes sense because it is a traditional way to greet someone.

5. **When you leave, say "It was nice to meet you."**
    The final step ensures that you end the interaction on a friendly note.

The teachers chose this particular skill because they commonly welcome dozens of new students throughout the academic year. They reasoned that as society becomes more mobile, students are more transient. It makes sense, then, that students should be able to introduce themselves to peers, teachers, and other adults in the building. The teachers broke down the skill into five sequential steps, and included a rationale for each step. Whenever they taught the steps of the skill, they shared the rationales with students so they understood why each step is important.

If you are trying to keep the steps manageable and understandable, you can't always spell out all the behaviors associated with doing each step. There are "paraskills," such as voice tone, eye contact, and body language, that influence a student's success at using a skill. They help define the quality of the interaction. Even if students follow all the steps of a skill, they may not be successful if their nonverbal behaviors send a contradictory message. Therefore, it's important to explain and model the paraskills you want to see from students. This will help them understand what you mean by "appropriate" or "pleasant." Here is an example: You catch Dominic talking to his neighbor, and you ask him to please be quiet and get back on task. The social skill Dominic needs to use is "Following Instructions." As Dominic does the steps of the skill, there are certain behaviors you want to see and some you don't:

GUIDELINES FOR TASK ANALYSIS

- Keep the focus of the skill limited.
- Identify behaviors of the skill as steps.
- Use specific and observable terms.
- Put steps in order of performance.

Following Instructions

Step 1
Dominic looks at you.

Behavior
Dominic makes eye contact. He doesn't roll his eyes, glare, or try to stare you down.

Step 2

Dominic says, "Okay."

> **Behavior**
>
> Dominic answers right away, and speaks clearly and pleasantly. He doesn't say, "Ooo-KAAAY," or use any condescending, snotty, or angry vocal inflection.

Step 3

Dominic follows your request immediately.

> **Behavior**
>
> Dominic stops talking, gets back on task, and completes his work. He doesn't respond by giving you an excuse or continuing to talk.

Step 4

Dominic checks back with you.

> **Behavior**
>
> Dominic raises his hand, tells you he's completed his assignment, and asks what he should work on next.

In an ideal world, Dominic responds to your instructions without defiance and his nonverbal behaviors are appropriate for the situation. Of course, that may not always be the case. That's why it's so important to model the same behaviors you expect from your students. Yelling back at them, rolling your eyes, or taking an aggressive posture only contributes to a negative, unhealthy environment. It can defeat the whole purpose of teaching students social skills.

How fast students learn a particular skill or how well they follow its behavioral steps will depend on their developmental level and their areas of strength and weakness. For example, some students are great at developing relationships with adults, but they struggle to hold conversations with their peers. Others are very good at working independently, but they can't get along with others when doing group work. You also have to consider context. We worked with a teacher who taught a speech class. At the start of the semester, one of his students reacted to his criticisms by arguing and turning her back on him. By the end of the semester, her response to his criticisms had been reduced to rolling her eyes and looking away. Her behaviors had evolved in a positive way over the semester, and while they may not have been "ideal" or matched his expectations, progress was made.

Like anything else you want students to learn, you can't simply talk about it once and move on. To be effective, you'll have to teach and practice the skills, then assess, redirect, and reinforce students' efforts. Clear, consistent social skills instruction will only increase the likelihood that your students learn new behaviors. In Chapter 11, we'll look at how you can take socials skills and incorporate them into your school day using a variety of teaching methods.

SOCIAL SKILLS RESOURCE

Fortunately, you don't have to figure out all the behavioral steps of every conceivable social skill on your own. *Teaching Social Skills to Youth: A Step-by-Step Guide to 182 Basic to Complex Skills* (Dowd and Tierney, 2005) does it for you. This is an excellent resource, and the behavioral examples used in this chapter come from that Boys Town book.

Final Thoughts

Social skills instruction is a universal intervention that offers benefits to all students. However, some youth, specifically those diagnosed as emotionally or behaviorally disturbed, will require more intensive and individualized intervention. For these students, social skills instruction alone may do little to alter behavior. Additional intervention strategies must complement the teaching of social skills and those efforts should involve the school psychologist, support personnel, and the child's parents or primary caregivers.

Multi-Tiered Systems of Support

According to a 2008 MetLife Survey on the American Teacher, 43% of teachers feel their classrooms are so mixed in terms of student learning and behavioral ability that they can't teach their students effectively. The behavioral challenges teachers face in today's classrooms require them to be able to meet students' behavioral needs at various levels, and unfortunately, an increased inability to manage these challenges has emerged. Additionally, in response to increased behavioral difficulties, many schools have implemented discipline policies to establish control, using increasingly aversive consequences such as "zero tolerance" and, for the most difficult students, expulsions. The assumption is that increasing the severity of consequences for repeated misbehavior will reduce or stop the problem; however, these practices have little impact on student behavior and often cause them to become more severe (Sugai & Horner, 2006; Skiba, & Peterson, 2000).

An alternative to this punitive approach is to establish a multi-tiered system of support at both the school and classroom level to meet students' behavioral needs. Various "frameworks" such as PBIS (Positive Behavior Interventions and Supports), RtI (Response to Intervention), and MTSS (Multi-Tiered Systems of Supports) have emerged in recent years to help schools and teachers take a more preventive approach to student behavior rather than the traditional reactive approach of waiting for students to fail. Research on these frameworks has shown that they increase student achievement, reduce discipline referrals, and improve school culture (Horner, Sugai, & Anderson, 2010). These frameworks also focus on the school as a unit, regularly assess student needs, apply multi-tiered systems of support, and provide these supports as early as possible (Horner et al., 2010).

Because these are frameworks, the emphasis is on a process or an approach rather than a curriculum, intervention, or practice. The "continuum" notion emphasizes how evidence- or research-based behavioral practices are organized within a multi-tiered system of support, also called "response to intervention" (Sugai & Horner, 2009). Boys Town's Well-Managed Schools program focuses on the idea of supporting students' needs at various levels by creating predictable environments, reinforcing positive behavior, and correcting behavior when it is minor. The program goes a step further than the frameworks listed earlier by providing schools and teachers with specific strategies to implement a multi-tiered system of support.

An effective multi-tiered system of support can be represented as a pyramid with three tiers of intervention: universal, or tier 1; secondary, or tier 2;, and tertiary, or tier 3. To establish this type of framework, it is important to define what each tier represents and how an intervention should be focused to enable a proactive approach to behavior.

Multi-Tiered System of Supports

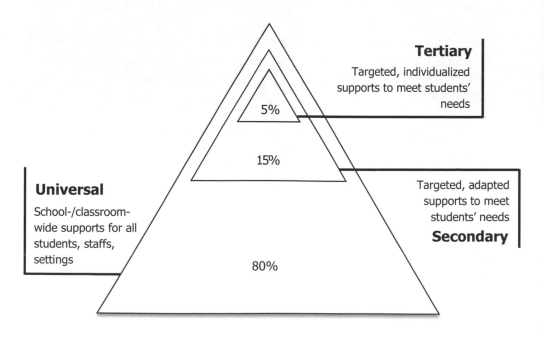

Universal Interventions

The bottom of the triangle represents universal (tier 1) interventions. These interventions are applied to all students, and schools tend to find that this level of support is sufficient for about 80 to 90 percent of students. Universal interventions take on a very proactive approach in that schools are encouraged to establish and implement a common language, common practices, and consistent application of positive and negative consequences that are applicable in all settings in and around the school. The goal of this level of intervention is to prevent new cases of problem behavior in the school. This layer of support typically has the following features:

- **Developing and teaching behavioral expectations.** This includes rules, routines, or procedures, and physical arrangements whose aim is to prevent occurrences of problem behaviors.

- **Labeling and teaching appropriate behavioral actions.** Many schools have adopted this approach by creating and displaying common expectations that outline examples of appropriate behavior in various areas of the school. Schools teach these expectations in a number of ways, but the emphasis should be on formalizing a schedule and format for teaching them.

- **Observing and praising appropriate behaviors.** There is a strong emphasis on catching kids being good and specifically describing the positive behaviors students display. Many schools also have adopted the recommendation to use some sort of token economy, along with reward schedules, to reinforce appropriate behavior.

Secondary Interventions

The next level of the pyramid is secondary (tier 2) interventions. When students struggle to find success at the universal intervention level, it is necessary to employ secondary interventions as an increased level of support. At the secondary level, interventions are more intensive and target a smaller portion of the student body. In fact, many schools find that only about 5 to 10 percent of their students fall into this category. These are students who tend to be at a higher risk for engaging in more serious negative behaviors.

At the secondary intervention level, student supports are different from universal supports because the focus of the supports is narrow and becomes more individualized and flexible. In this manner, secondary supports often aim to provide targeted group interventions to 10 or more students and may include specific interventions like social skills groups, check-ins/check-outs, Behavior Education Plans, Functional Behavioral Assessments, and environmental changes. These secondary level supports seek to reduce current incidents of problem behavior, improvements that can be measured through the use of direct observations and progress monitoring. Some of the key features of secondary interventions include:

- **Continuous availability and rapid access to supports.** Many of these supports will be delivered via small groups multiple times per week, possibly daily (e.g., check-ins/check-outs). If the need for interventions unexpectedly arises, they should be readily available.

- **Very low effort by teachers.** Interventions should be based on what the teacher is currently doing in the classroom, but should be more targeted for a student or a group of students to increase their buy-in.

- **Implemented by all staff/faculty in a school and consistent with school-wide expectations.** All staff members who have contact with students should know the interventions and how to implement them. This increases predictability and positive outcomes for the students.

- **Flexible interventions based on assessment.** Implementation of this type of intervention should be based on data gathered through interviews and direct observation; interventions then can be adjusted to fit student achievement (more time in class, fewer office discipline referrals, increased rates of being on task) with the goal of "stepping down" supports.

- **Continuous monitoring of student behavior for decision making.**

Tertiary Interventions

Tertiary (tier 3) interventions become necessary when students exhibit patterns of problem behavior that are dangerous, highly disruptive, and impede learning, resulting in social or educational exclusion. Tertiary interventions are typically individual supports that target 1 to 5 percent of the student body in a school. The goal of these interventions is to reduce the complications and the severity/intensity of current cases of problem behavior and, in many cases, teach students social skills at an individual level, which promotes success in life and enhances the students' quality of life. This level of intervention often occurs after a school conducts a Functional Behavioral Assessment (FBA) with the primary purpose of:

- **Identifying goals of the intervention.** This should be based on available behavioral information and incorporate goals for eventually stepping down supports.

- **Gathering relevant information.** This includes examining a student's history of interventions and records, and conducting direct observations of behavior patterns.

- **Developing summary statements.** These statements describe the relationship between a student's behaviors of concern and environmental elements.

- **Generating a behavioral support plan that outlines how to achieve the goals.** This should include:

  — Making environmental adaptations that serve to prevent problem behavior

  — Teaching replacement skills and building general competencies

  — Using consequences that reinforce positive behavior and reduce problem behavior

  — Developing a crisis management plan (if needed)

- **Implementing and monitoring outcomes.** This includes designating resources, including staff, training, time, and physical resources. Communication, assessment, and adjustment also are crucial to the long-term success of the plan.

Tertiary interventions provide additional reinforcement to the interventions students may be receiving at the secondary and/or universal levels, increasing student motivation to change and/or reduce their negative behaviors. When a student's behavior improves, the level of support should be reduced. If the level of support is too high, a student's negative behavior often will increase rather than decrease because of the amount of attention the student is receiving. It is important to eventually fade supports to help students generalize behavior and maintain growth over time.

Final Thoughts

Boys Town's Well-Managed Schools program provides schools with specific teaching strategies for supporting their students through a range of interventions to address behavioral concerns. The program provides common language and common standards for behavior as teachers learn and use Boys Town's social skills and strategies for teaching students appropriate behavior. Teachers learn to share a common approach when teaching social skills in a preventive manner, when reinforcing appropriate use of social skills and positive behaviors, and when correcting inappropriate student behavior. As mentioned earlier, the program equips teachers with identifiable preventive, reinforcement, and corrective strategies across several levels of support to meet the individual needs of students in their classrooms. The Well-Managed Schools program provides a great foundation on which teachers and schools can build a system of sustainable behavioral supports to increase students' positive behavior, regardless of the students' level of functioning. The following chapters will outline the details of how to use these strategies as a multi-tiered system of support within the program.

Teaching Social Skills

Many of the students who walk into your classroom will lack the social skills necessary to consistently find success in school. Even when you take the time to teach about rules, procedures, and consequences, some students will struggle, make mistakes, and act out. Most simply do not have all the information or tools they need to make the best choices. As their teacher, you are in a special position to help students by teaching them the social skills necessary to achieve success, in the classroom and ultimately in life. While this may seem daunting, it is doable!

Fortunately, many educators recognize the importance of social skills and embrace the challenge of teaching young people the skills they'll need to achieve school success. However, we've also heard more than a few teachers argue that social skills instruction is not their job. They tell us it's the responsibility of parents. Others complain about not having enough time to get through their lesson plans; they say talking about social skills only "wastes" time they do not have. We've even heard secondary school teachers blame their peers at the elementary level for not doing enough when it really could have made a difference. In high school, they say, it's too late. We know, of course, that it's never too early or too late to show young people how to take control of their lives.

To say that teaching social skills is the sole responsibility of parents doesn't make much sense. We know there are countless young people who come from dysfunctional families or no families at all. Some of these students enter school with behaviors they've adopted or learned from the streets and other difficult environments. Many of these learned behaviors and attitudes are not what you want to see in your classroom or school. Unless they are taught alternative behaviors, these students will do what they know – good, bad, or indifferent. Others may have idyllic home lives, yet they still have limited social skills or simply can't adapt or transfer those skills to the classroom.

Regardless of the experiences and environments students have outside of school, social skills instruction can be a great equalizer because it empowers each individual to be more successful regardless of the circumstances.

In this chapter, we'll examine several preventive teaching strategies that you can use to introduce social skills to your students. One involves integrating skills into existing lesson plans and homework assignments, thereby eliminating one often-heard objection (or excuse): There's not enough time in the school day!

Preventive Social Skills Instruction

Before you can preventively teach social skills, you need some understanding of what skills your students lack or need to improve. One way you can prioritize the skills you teach is to review the 16 social skills identified in Chapter 9. They serve as the foundation for a healthy learning environment, so making sure your students develop and improve the use of those skills is a great place to begin. Other strategies you can employ to assess the skills of your students include personal observations and interactions, office referral data, and informal conversations with staff, students, and parents.

Personal observations and interactions provide the most immediate feedback. Being attentive to what's happening in the classrooms, hallways, cafeteria, and common areas will often reveal the skill levels and abilities of students. The social skills you choose to emphasize should be based on the behaviors you're seeing. Office referral data is also helpful in identifying any behavioral problems – bullying, verbal aggression, vandalism, frequent tardiness, etc. – students commonly or consistently struggle with. Using information gleaned from office referrals, you can develop intervention strategies and target social skills to address the problem behaviors. Throughout this book, we've emphasized the importance of taking an ecological or whole-school perspective. To get a big-picture point of view, it's helpful to not only review office referrals, but also to have conversations with stakeholders, especially parents and other staff. These individuals are good sources of information about problems (some of which you may be unaware of) and getting their help can make your intervention efforts more successful.

As you evaluate the behavioral needs of students, keep in mind that your level of interest in emphasizing and teaching certain social skills may be much higher than that of your students.

For example, you may believe that the skill of "Accepting 'No' for an Answer" is essential for a well-managed school. However, some of your students may be reluctant to follow the behavioral steps you've outlined for that skill. They may be embarrassed or afraid to follow the steps, fearing they'll lose status with their peers. The manner in which you select and teach social skills should take the child's perspective into consideration, along with your own, for the greatest impact and effectiveness (Tierney, Green, & Dowd, 2016).

Preventive Teaching Strategies

Once you assess the needs of your students (keep in mind this should be a continual process that goes on throughout the academic year), you can teach social skills much like you would any other content area. Teaching skills preventively (before students need to use them) is a way for you to introduce new social skills to students, reinforce the skills they are learning, and prepare students for future situations where they will need to use specific skills or behaviors. Here are three teaching methods we recommend for preventive social skills instruction:

- Planned Teaching

- Blended Teaching

- Preventive Prompting

How to Use Planned Teaching

Planned Teaching is a strategy in which you systematically introduce students to a new social skill (or a classroom rule or expectation) at a planned, neutral time. The purpose of Planned Teaching is to prepare students for specific situations or circumstances that may be new to them or were difficult for them in the past. Planned Teaching can be done one-on-one with students, in small groups, or with an entire class. When it is used for social skills instruction, Planned Teaching looks like this:

1. **Introduce the skill.**
2. **Describe the appropriate behavior.**
3. **Give a reason.**
4. **Practice.**

1. **Introduce the skill.** First, label the skill you are going to teach ("Accepting Criticism" or "Disagreeing Appropriately") and carefully describe situations in which the skill can be used. Give students multiple, specific examples of the skill so they can see how it is used in different contexts. Here is how introducing a skill in your classroom might sound:

   "Today, we're going to talk about how to introduce yourself to someone you have never met or maybe haven't seen in a long time. This is a social skill we call 'Greeting Others.' Everyone think about a time when you introduced yourself to someone. Be ready to share your experience with the class."

2. **Describe the appropriate behavior.** In Chapter 9, we showed you how a group of teachers task-analyzed the skill, "Introducing Yourself." In this phase of Planned Teaching, you essentially do the same thing, identifying and describing the behavioral steps required to perform the skill. As you describe the behaviors, clearly state what you expect to see from students so they can achieve the best results. You may have to spend time defining terms, discussing exceptions or special circumstances (greeting a new classmate may look and sound different than greeting a distant relative or new principal), and teaching certain behaviors, or "paraskills," that complement the individual steps. Here is how you might describe the behavioral steps of "Introducing Yourself" to students:

   "Class, the first step in 'Introducing Yourself' is to look at the person and smile. The next step is to use a pleasant tone of voice and offer a greeting, such as 'Hi, my name is…." Then, shake the person's hand. Finally, when you end the interaction, say to the person, 'It was nice to meet you.'"

   When describing the behavioral steps, remind students that a skill may not always look the same when the circumstances or people involved change. To help broaden their perspective of what a skill might look like, ask students questions that force them to think how the steps of a skill might change depending on the situation. In other words, what can they do to use the skill better or more naturally in different environments? For example, you might say something like this: "Let's talk about shaking someone's hand. When do you think you would or wouldn't do that? What might you do instead? What would you do if the other person didn't extend his or her hand?" By giving students a variety of different contexts to consider, you help them generalize the use of the skill to different settings and conditions.

3. **Give a reason.** Reasons provide a cognitive connection between the skill or behavior and its consequences. When students know why or how certain behaviors or skills are beneficial or helpful, they are more likely to use them. As we explained earlier in this book, reasons make the most sense when they point out one of three things – benefits to the students, possible negative outcomes, or benefits to others. We sometimes refer to these different reasons as the three H's because they answer one of three questions:

   • How does using this skill help me?

   • How does not using this skill hurt me?

   • How does using this skill help others?

   The type of reason you use with students may depend on their age, attitude, or whatever you believe will have the most meaning to them. For example, you might tell a painfully shy student that when he introduces himself to other people, they are more likely to want to talk to him (benefit to self). Or, you might tell an entire class that when they introduce themselves to new students and staff, they make the newcomers feel welcome (benefit to others). When discussing the reasons for using a particular skill, encourage students to come up with some on their own. Their reasons are likely to be more meaningful and personally motivating than reasons that are spoon-fed to them by a teacher.

4. **Practice the skill.** This step means you get students actively involved in demonstrating the skill or showing how it

can be used in various situations. This can be done through role-plays, demonstrations, games, art lessons, music, writing exercises, or any other creative outlet. Having students practice a skill is important because it lets you see how well they translate the skill into observable actions and whether or not you should adjust your teaching methods. Practicing a skill can be done by having students work in pairs (so everyone gets a chance to participate), small groups (so additional skills such as "Having a Conversation" can be practiced), or individually (on their own at home or with the teacher). Regardless of how a skill is practiced, it's important that students be monitored so practice time is used constructively and not for goofing off or tuning out.

If a practice session goes well, or you notice students using the social skills they've learned, you may want to acknowledge their efforts with a positive consequence. Remember, a positive consequence is anything that reinforces good behaviors. If you're working one-on-one with a student, you might give him or her a pat on the back or say, "Awesome effort!" If you're working with a group, it's important that everyone – not just some members of the group – engaged in appropriate behaviors. Group behaviors that can be recognized or praised include staying on task, making positive comments, practicing the skill, and participating. The consequence a group earns for good behavior should reflect their needs or developmental level. Possible rewards might include extra recess or computer time, homework passes, or free time to talk with friends.

How to Use Blended Teaching

A second strategy for preventively teaching skills involves blending or combining social skill and academic instruction. Blended teaching is a teacher's intentional integration of a social/emotional skill and the content of an academic lesson.

Unlike Planned Teaching, blended teaching is an integrated process where social skills are connected to the actual academic content. This is when you connect social skills to the content being taught, whether the subject is English, economics, electronic media, or something else. In one California history class, for example, students learned about the life and work of César Chávez. As part of the discussion, students had to write about an experience in which they or someone they knew stood up for or defended a cause, belief, or individual. In their essays, the students had to identify the different skills – showing perseverance, resiliency, or respect – they or others demonstrated. A Georgia elementary school also found a creative way to use blended teaching. Each week during Black History Month, the school honored a prominent African-American while emphasizing a social skill that related to the honoree's life or career. During Thurgood Marshall week, the skill of "Listening to Others" was highlighted. For Rosa Parks, the skill was "Resisting Peer Pressure."

These examples illustrate how blended teaching incorporates social skills into the school day as part of the academic lessons. When you are able to connect social and emotional skills into everyday discussions, it helps students generalize skills and connect social learning outside the classroom. In addition, it helps make teaching social skills more natural and less prescriptive, making the process easier for teachers. Blended teaching is often easiest to implement for ELA teachers because stories often connect with social and emotional learning. However, blended teaching also can be used in special-area classes or even science and math. For example, when a physical education teacher introduces a lesson on basketball, baseball, or soccer, he can talk about teamwork and the importance of everyone having a role. This is a great way to connect the social skill of "Working with Others" with the academic content of the class. In science, if a teacher is discussing volcanoes and plate tectonics, this is a great place for her to lead a discussion on bullying and controlling one's emotions, tying emotion-

BLENDED TEACHING EXAMPLES

Here are two scenarios that highlight ways you can blend social skills instruction with academic instruction:

In an Introduction to Psychology class, students are making Rorschach inkblot tests with paper and paint. You explain to the students that there are many methods for analyzing one's attitude toward life and that the class is experimenting with one of them. You tell your students, "We are going to talk about how to appropriately share your ideas and attitudes."

You are teaching a literature lesson around the book, *Holes*. In the story, Stanley Yelnats is the victim of mistaken identity who winds up doing time in a juvenile detention home. Stanley and the other inmates are made to dig holes by a warden who tells them it "builds character." Students are going to explore the meaning of "character" and identify examples in the book where someone demonstrated good or bad character. You tell your students, "Let's talk about ways you can show others at school you're a person of character."

al outbursts to volcanic explosions and explaining how using coping skills or self-control strategies can help manage emotions.

Blended teaching is a concept that is sometimes easier to understand than to use. Some teachers have an innate sense of knowing the right time to relate a social skill to an academic lesson and can do it on the fly. But for most, blended teaching requires planning and thoughtful reflection. The most common missteps we see teachers make include focusing on a skill that doesn't relate to the material being discussed, introducing a skill so abruptly that it confuses students, and spending so much time on a skill, the subject matter becomes secondary.

Fortunately, these potential pitfalls can be avoided simply by being aware of them. Always think about where skill teaching will fit in best, and understand that you don't need to have a long, involved discussion. In fact, the more focused your remarks are, the more likely it is that your students will understand the connection you're making. Again, the purpose of blended teaching is to make social skills more real and relevant to students' everyday lives. The more you can help them see how social skills work in the real world, the more engaged and interested they will be to learn them.

How to Use Preventive Prompting

The preventive prompt is a brief reminder or statement about the use of a skill just prior to the event or situation in which a student needs to use the skill. Typically, you transition from Planned Teaching or blended teaching strategies to preventive prompts. As students gain more experience and demonstrate mastery of a particular skill or situation, specific skill teaching can be phased out. Examples of preventive prompts include asking a student, "Do you remember the steps to following instructions?" just before instructing the student to clean the blackboard, or saying, "Remember the steps we talked about for leaving the building during a fire drill" as the alarm begins to sound.

Preventive prompts are not "after-the-fact" statements. In other words, if a student fails to follow a particular instruction you've given, a proactive response would not be, "Now, remember what I said about following instructions." That's actually a corrective prompt (see Chapter 13). Preventive prompts are a proactive way to remind students of a behavioral expectation and to set them up for success **BEFORE** they take an action.

Keep in mind that when individual students struggle with a skill or in certain situations, a preventive prompt will not give them the direction or help they need. If an entire class regresses and inappropriate behaviors start reoccurring, a preventive prompt won't be enough to correct the changing dynamic. You may have to go back to more Planned Teaching or blended teaching. Sometimes it's wise to reassess your whole approach. Are you teaching the right skills? Do other skills need to be re-taught? Should you change how you teach the skills? Can changing the classroom/school rules or procedures make a difference? Are you using consequences effectively? Are you reinforcing (through praise or other positive consequences) the good choices students make or do you only focus on their mistakes? All of these issues should be reconsidered whenever problem behaviors become more frequent or intense.

Teaching for Generalization and Code Switching

Generalization and code switching are similar, but there is a subtle distinction between the two. Generalization is when students can successfully use the steps of a social skill regardless of the environment (the behavioral steps look the same; the environment changes). Code switching is when students can successfully alter the behavioral steps to best reflect the different circumstances and relationships they encounter (the steps look different in different contexts).

While the entire preventive teaching process helps students use social skills in various situations, there are a few other methods worth noting. The best way for students to learn any skill is through practice. By practicing, they can "over-learn" a skill, which hopefully is what happens. It means students can use a skill regardless of the environment, and use it effectively regardless of the conditions. To help students "over-learn" a skill, we recommend these three techniques:

Practice in different settings. Match the skill you're teaching with a real environment. If you're working on appropriate cafeteria behavior, take your students to the lunchroom. Take them through the process of standing in line, asking for food, walking to their tables, and cleaning up. You want to put them in the position where they can actually see how they can use the skills you're teaching. The more realistic and relevant the scenario, the more powerful the learning experience will be for them.

Practice with different people. Students might be able to generalize skills more easily and quickly if they're learning from different people. Whenever possible, include those who will be directly involved with your students in different contexts. If you're teaching students about good sportsmanship, involve the school's coaches or playground aides. If you're teaching students how to handle stress, you might involve a school counselor or nurse. When practicing with someone else is not possible, it's important to show students how a skill might or should look when used with other people. For instance, if you are teaching students how to follow instructions, you will teach them to look at the person, say "Okay," and do what the person says right away. In addition, you'll want to make sure they know this is how the skill should look if any adult in the building – a principal, secretary, nurse, substitute teacher, etc. – asks them to do something.

Give "homework" assignments. Just like with academics, the use of social skills homework can help students retain and generalize new information. Ask students to try out a particular social skill with a friend, family member, or other adult. Then have them record the results and share their experience with the class.

Multi-Tiered Systems of Support

Using preventive strategies is a great way to reduce behavioral concerns for students at the individual, classroom, and school levels. However, students will need varying levels of support. The preventive strategies in the Well-Managed Schools program are flexible in implementation and designed to provide students support at the universal, secondary, and tertiary levels. You can think of these as a continuum of support with the focus becoming more targeted and individualized as the need increases. The following graphic represents the preventive strategies in a multi-tiered system of support:

Universal Interventions

- Set clear, specific behavioral expectations before problems occur.

- Develop a "Skill of the Week" for a school-wide focus.

- Teach social skills to introduce new skills or prevent problematic behaviors.

- Apply expectations consistently.

- Use whole-group Planned Teaching to teach expectations, procedures, and skills.

- Blend academic content and social skill instruction.

- Use preventive prompts to reinforce expectations.

Secondary Interventions

- Use more frequent Planned Teaching and individual preventive prompts.

- Organize social skills groups.

- Identify a peer model who can practice social skills with a student under adult supervision.

- Collaborate with outside resources to practice skills in small-group settings, when necessary.

Tertiary Interventions

- Identify and use specific and individualized targeted skills to address a student's needs.

- Increase the frequency of individualized Planned Teaching that is focused on targeted skills.

- Collaborate with outside supports (counselor, therapist, parents, special education staff, student assistance team, etc.) to increase individualized prevention.

- Provide frequent individualized preventive prompts.

Final Thoughts

All of the strategies and teaching methods outlined in this chapter and throughout Section II are designed to set students up for success. They are a way for you to be proactive and build relationships with your students so some problem behaviors can be completely avoided and others won't be so severe or frequent. Of course, there will be times when students will act out or lose control. In Section III, we look at how you can respond to both the good and the bad behaviors of students.

Addressing
Student Behavior

I N SECTION I, THE EMPHASIS WAS ON CONNECTING WITH students by communicating warmth, showing concern, and modeling respect. Section II focused on creating an environment where students have more opportunities to succeed by defining expectations, setting boundaries, and creating consistency. When such preventive measures are adopted in one's learning community, students find themselves immersed in a culture that celebrates the individual and values appropriate behavior. As a result, the whole environment is one where "all students know what is required for behavioral success, and where students encourage appropriate behavior from each other" (Horner et al., 2001, p. 94).

Still, even the most structured and supportive environments cannot escape challenging moments. Students will get off task, act out, and disrupt your teaching. In the next three chapters, we look at ways to recognize and respond to both the disruptive and constructive behaviors of students.

Acknowledging the good things students do, including their social and academic progress, is the focus of Chapter 12. Healthy social climates accentuate the positive. It does little good to concentrate solely on correcting problem behaviors if no effort is made to praise and support students when they make good decisions.

Dealing with students' behavioral mistakes and moving past them in a constructive way is the focus of the final two chapters of Section III. In Chapter 13, several intervention strategies to address inappropriate behaviors are explained. These techniques give you multiple options for handling students whose behaviors range from the distracting to the disruptive. You'll also learn why success depends on correcting and changing the behavior, not placing blame. Finally, Chapter 14 tackles the problem of students who become emotionally intense. Behavior correction approaches that calm and redirect students so they can make better choices are explained step-by-step, using real classroom scenarios.

CHAPTER

Encouraging Positive Behaviors

When a teacher told us she didn't believe in praising her students, we had to ask why. "Grades should motivate my students, not me," she shot back. Her opinion was straightforward, but disappointingly misguided.

Grades certainly can be a great motivator for many students, especially if playing on an athletic team depends on having a certain grade point or if earning a scholarship to a prestigious college requires more A's than C's. But not every student cares about grades. And even if all students were motivated by their grades, that doesn't necessarily mean they will be models of good behavior in the classroom. There are plenty of class clowns and bullies who achieve academic success in spite of the grief and chaos they cause in the classroom and to their classmates.

When it comes to changing and improving the behaviors of students, praise is one of the most powerful tools you have, and it should be a major part of every school day. Praise is crucial to the development of positive relationships between you and your students, and, when used appropriately, can reinforce and encourage appropriate behaviors.

There are different types of praise and different ways it can be communicated to students. For example, general praise is a positive verbal statement ("Awesome job!") or nonverbal gesture (thumbs-up) you give a student when he or she engages in appropriate behavior. For many students, general praise is easily understood and offers enough encouragement and reinforcement for them to continue to act in an appropriate manner in your classroom. Other students require a little more help in understanding exactly why they are being praised. For them, specific praise is useful. Specific praise is when you take a general praise statement and pair it with a description of the behavior. It can sound something like this: "Way to go! You answered all of the test questions." The use of both general and specific praise can increase the likelihood that your students will continue to engage in appropriate behavior. Both also are appropriate ways to acknowledge the academic successes of students.

Just as specific praise provides more details than general praise because it links praise to a behavior, a third type of praise offers even more specificity. We call it Effective Praise.

What Is Effective Praise?

Effective Praise is your enthusiastic response to students when you catch them being good or giving great effort. This completely positive interaction acknowledges and reinforces their efforts to engage in and maintain appropriate behaviors. Using Effective Praise is a four-step process that is purposeful, specific, and genuine. Most importantly, it is dependent on positive behavior. Making Effective Praise truly effective requires you to recognize good behaviors when they happen, describe those behaviors in concrete terms, and then link those behaviors to positive outcomes. When you acknowledge the appropriate behaviors your students demonstrate in the classroom, you make it more likely those behaviors will be repeated.

How to Use Effective Praise

Effective Praise should be given only after a desired behavior occurs, not as a general motivator. By offering praise after a student demonstrates a particular behavior, you attribute success to that student's effort. This, in turn, lets the student know that similar success can be attained again. You want the student to realize that he or she is in charge and in control of his or her own behavior.

Effective Praise should explicitly state which behaviors are being recognized and reinforced. Simple, direct statements will enhance a student's understanding of what is being praised, and lend credibility to the interaction. Recognizing developmental levels and individual needs when praising students personalizes the interactions and shows students you are sincere.

The Steps of Effective Praise

Before discussing the steps of Effective Praise, it is necessary to emphasize an important aspect of this and other interactions you will have with your students. Whenever you talk with students about their behaviors, you communicate not only with your words, but also with your actions. How you talk with someone often is considerably more important than what you actually say. Because of this, you should pay close attention to factors called "quality components." Basically, these components refer to your positive verbal and nonverbal behaviors. They include looking at the student, using a pleasant voice tone, saying the student's name, smiling, using appropriate humor, and showing enthusiasm. High-fives and touching, such as a pat on the shoulder, also can be used, but with obvious caution. Of course, your use of touch will be based on many factors and will vary from one student to another.

Quality components establish and maintain a productive climate for learning. In general, everyone is more receptive to teaching when they are approached in a positive manner. In any teaching interaction, but especially when you're correcting students, using positive behaviors at the start and maintaining them throughout is beneficial.

You should feel comfortable and natural when talking to students about their behavior; students will not respond well to an adult who appears insincere or "robotic." In fact, when young people perceive praise as insincere or dishonest, they tend to dismiss it (Henderlong & Lepper, 2002). When used naturally and spontaneously, quality components can greatly improve the relationships between you and your students.

Here are the steps of Effective Praise:

1. **Show approval.**

   As mentioned earlier, this can be done in any number of ways. Verbal statements such as "Good job," "Awesome try," "Nice work," "Super effort," or "Excellent" are verbal ways of expressing your appreciation. You can also communicate nonverbally by showing a thumbs-up, giving a high-five, applauding, smiling, or giving a pat on the back. Always try to look happy and be enthusiastic when showing approval. You want students to see that you care about their success and want them to succeed.

2. Describe the appropriate behavior.

Effective Praise combines specific behavioral statements with your general praise and enthusiasm. Descriptions of appropriate behavior increase a student's level of understanding and the likelihood that he or she will repeat the behavior. These statements help students realize exactly what behaviors fall within the acceptable range. They also help students focus on their accomplishments and progress.

STEPS OF EFFECTIVE PRAISE

1. Show approval.

2. Describe the appropriate behavior.

3. Give a reason.

4. Use a positive consequence.
   (Tangible consequences are optional.)

As with any clear description of behavior, describe specific circumstances surrounding the behavior – what happened, who was there, when it happened, how it happened, and so on. (Be careful not to get so descriptive that you bring up irrelevant or minor facts and lose a student's attention.) Again, clear descriptions help teach students how to generalize appropriate behavior to similar situations and provide context for your description.

As you make descriptive praise statements, accurately label the skill you are reinforcing: "Thanks for looking at me, saying 'Okay,' and getting your book out when I asked. You did a good job of following instructions." Labeling skills and providing specific behavioral descriptions increases the odds that students will successfully learn new ways of behaving and be able to generalize the skill to future situations.

Specifically describe the skill steps performed correctly by the student. Here is an example, "When I told you that you couldn't use the calculator, you looked at me, said 'Okay,' and then calmly asked for a reason why. You did a good job of accepting a 'No' answer."

3. Give a reason.

Students benefit from learning about the consequences of their behavior. A rationale emphasizes this cause-effect relationship. Realistic, individualized rationales let students know why a specific behavior is beneficial to them or others. To your benefit, students will view you as more concerned and fair. Rationales also can help with compliance – students are more likely to do as they're asked when given a reason for doing so. And finally, rationales increase the pleasantness of interactions and are a key to building positive relationships with students. Here is an example: "When you appropriately accept a 'No' answer like you just did, others may be more likely to say 'Yes' to your requests in the future."

As with any interaction you have, make sure the student is paying attention and understands your rationale. Ask for an acknowledgement. Good questions to ask include, "Do you understand?" or "Does that make sense?" or "Do you follow me?" Requesting acknowledgement creates a dialogue, and should take place frequently during any teaching moment.

4. **Use a positive consequence.** (Tangible consequences are optional.)

Positive consequences help promote constructive, rapid behavior change when paired with specific skill teaching. Tell the student what positive consequences he or she earned for engaging in the specific appropriate behavior. For example, "Midori, you did such a good job of accepting 'No' for an answer, you've earned three extra minutes of independent time," or "You handled that disagreement in your cooperative group so well, you may choose a reading buddy during center time."

Positive consequences are effective because they strengthen and reinforce the behavior. To help ensure that the consequence or reward has the desired effect, it must be individualized to the student and appropriate for the situation. For example, a student who enjoys recess might be reinforced by earning extra recess time; but if a student doesn't enjoy recess, such a reward would not be positive. On the other hand, one student may enjoy passing out papers to the class, but another student might find it too embarrassing. As the teacher, you have to develop a relationship with each of your students so you know what motivates them.

In addition, the size of the reward or reinforcer must be appropriate; it should be just large enough to maintain or increase the positive behavior. Remember, there are many kinds of positive reinforcers, from tangibles (stickers, marbles, toys) to activities (passing out papers, running an errand, working on the computer), to social reinforcers ("Awesome job!", smiles, high-fives). Use the reinforcer that you believe the student will enjoy or one that has demonstrated a positive effect on his or her behavior in the past. For example, some students only need social reinforcement to maintain their behavior: the interaction they have with you is, by itself, positively reinforcing. The one-on-one attention you give them during Steps 1 through 3 is enough of a reward. They don't require any additional motivation to maintain their behavior. Other students, however, may require more than a kind word. They need additional motivation, which can come from tangible rewards.

Here are examples of what Effective Praise can look like, depending on the age or developmental level of a student:

Example 1

Chase is a seventh-grade student in your class. He frequently has difficulty turning assignments in on time, so you have been working with him in this area. Today, Chase turned in his homework from last night and just finished his math assignment with the rest of the class.

1. Show approval.

   "Chase, you've really been working hard!"

2. Describe the appropriate behavior.

   "First thing this morning, you handed in your homework, and just now you finished your math paper right on time. Great job!"

3. Give a reason.

   "By doing assignments on time, you can practice what you just learned and get more of the assignment right because it's fresh in your mind. Then you can move on to the next thing."

4. Use a positive consequence.

   "For turning your assignments in on time, you've earned the privilege of being first in line for lunch. Way to go!"

When using a positive consequence, remember it must be individualized to fit the student's needs. If being first in line means nothing to Chase, maybe a better alternative would be to let him choose who he wants to have as a study partner that day. Positive reinforcement has to involve something the student likes or enjoys.

Example 2

Sarah is in your second-grade classroom this year. She is most often quiet and shy, participating minimally in class discussions. Today, during opening activities, she shared some information about her baby brother. After opening, when the other children have started their journal entries, you go over to talk with Sarah.

1. Show approval.

    "Sarah, thanks for telling us about your baby brother this morning during opening."

2. Describe the appropriate behavior.

    "You raised your hand, then used a voice that everyone could hear."

3. Give a reason.

    "Sharing in a group can be scary, but it helps others get to know you and gives you things to talk about later, too."

4. Use a positive consequence.

    "Since you did such a nice job of sharing in group, you can pick out a sticker for your chart."

Example 3

Pedro is a high school junior in your algebra class. He usually likes to work alone. Today, a new student joined your class, and Pedro offered to explain the in-class assignment to him. You wait to talk to Pedro after the new student begins working on the assignment (so you don't interrupt or interfere with their interaction).

1. Show approval.

    "That was an awesome idea, Pedro!"

2. Describe the appropriate behavior.

   "You volunteered to help our new student, and you used a pleasant voice tone and pulled the chair over for him."

3. Give a reason.

   "When you volunteer to help a new student, you make him feel welcome and part of our class."

4. Use a positive consequence.

   "Thanks, Pedro, for volunteering."

For Pedro, the positive social interaction he had with you and your verbal reinforcement was enough for him to continue to engage in positive classroom behaviors. No additional reinforcement is necessary.

When to Use Effective Praise

Use Effective Praise frequently to reinforce new skills or strengthen skills that are difficult. When students are learning something new, they need reinforcement every time they use the skill correctly. Continuous reinforcement builds and strengthens skills. By reinforcing the use of a skill that is just emerging, you increase the likelihood that the skill will be used again. Skills are developed more quickly, giving students a broader range of appropriate behaviors from which to draw.

Effective Praise should also be used when you are attempting to strengthen existing positive behaviors or build the fluency of a skill. As a student demonstrates more frequent and appropriate use of a skill, you should use an intermittent schedule of reinforcement to maintain the skill or behavior. Remember that the "element of surprise" (not knowing when a behavior will be reinforced) actually increases the chances that the student will use the skill. Using an intermittent schedule also helps with fading, which means gradually reducing the use of specific statements or tangible rewards.

Effective Praise shouldn't replace your use of general or specific praise. The type and frequency of praise should depend on how well a student maintains appropriate behavior. Once a behavior seems well established, you can fade out the use of specific descriptions and use general statements such as "Good job," "Nice work on the project," and so on. Keep in mind that if you never offer praise, the student may stop using the desired behavior. Also, behavior that was previously reinforced may diminish or cease if it isn't occasionally recognized or addressed. In general, established behaviors are best maintained when intermittent reinforcement is used. The ultimate goal of Effective Praise is to develop and maintain behavior through social interactions.

Benefits of Effective Praise

Effective Praise is a way to spotlight the good things your students are doing, which helps them learn and grow. Oftentimes, young people have difficulty developing constructive relationships with authority figures or making and keeping friends. Through Effective Praise, you can break down barriers and build more positive relationships with all of your students.

Many students will engage in behaviors that are noticed by others in order to gain approval. Although many of these behaviors could be considered prosocial, you need to guard against "programming" students to merely be obedient or compliant. Instead, you want to develop a sense of responsibility in your students. Show them the benefits of their positive behaviors so they can begin to develop an internalized set of values and motivations that will result in a sense of personal power (Miller, 1984). Students who act only to please others remain motivated by external factors, have trouble connecting outcomes to their behavior, and may be ill-prepared to function in the wider world (Bluestein, 2001).

Studies suggest that youth prefer being taught by adults who give positive feedback, set clear expectations with reasons to back them up, and show enthusiasm and concern. Similarly, studies have shown that students are more positive and friendly with others in their classrooms and develop more positive "attitudes" when they experience warm and accepting relationships with their teachers (Prawat & Nickerson, 1985; Solomon, Watson, Delucchi, Schaps, & Battistich, 1988). Effective Praise is designed to meet your students' needs and facilitate better relationships with them.

As you focus on what a student is doing well, you become more aware of the student's positive behaviors, creating a positive cycle of interactions. The more you are aware of what the student does "right," the more opportunities you have to address and increase positive behavior change. By learning and using skills that fit societal norms, students increase their range of behavioral responses and begin choosing those that are more readily accepted by others. In the end, Effective Praise increases learning and students' behavioral options.

Additional Considerations

Your teaching has the greatest impact when it closely follows a behavior. Relevant, immediate feedback enhances learning. There may be times, however, when you don't observe a positive behavior but still can praise a student for the choices he or she made. In these cases, you'll need to rely on other sources of information and talk with the student as soon as you can. For example, another teacher might tell you she saw one of your students appropriately disagreeing with another student instead of arguing or fighting. In this situation, get as much information as you can, then praise the student for the appropriate behavior.

Most often, you will use Effective Praise privately with a student. This provides complete and personal attention. Public praise can sometimes be appropriate, but it also can be embarrassing to a student and have counterproductive effects. Public praise should be reserved for situations when the entire class has demonstrated a skill or when you know a particular student will appreciate such recognition.

Positive interactions with students, including all three forms of praise, should occur at least four times as often as corrective interactions. This 4-to-1 ratio helps strengthen teacher-student relationships and results in more positive behaviors from students (Burke et al., 2007). By emphasizing the good things your students do, you help them focus on their positive actions and make them feel more competent and better about themselves.

The benefits of accentuating the positive extend beyond the classroom. Studies show that marriages are more successful and work groups are more productive when positive interactions exceed negative ones (Gottman, 1998; Fredrickson & Losada, 2005). Increasing your use of verbal and nonverbal affirmations with students can improve their productivity by increasing their on-task behaviors. The 4-to-1 ratio is a minimum standard; many of your students may need higher ratios of positive-to-corrective feedback to show improvement.

Multi-Tiered Systems of Support

An earlier discussion described how preventive strategies can be used as a multi-tiered system of support. Reinforcement can be used in the same way. Teachers have the ability to fade the type and amount of reinforcement based on a student's needs. Think of the strategies of reinforcement as a continuum; when students are just learning a skill or need support with mastering it, use a higher rate and specific type of reinforcement: then fade reinforcement based on the student's progress and needs. Some students will need a large amount of continuous reinforcement to sustain positive behavior; many students will need only intermittent reinforcement. Additionally, Effective Praise provides the largest, most impactful reinforcement for students at the highest level of need and can be combined with a motivation system or other reinforcement, if necessary. If a positive reinforcement like a tangible reward or a PBIS-type of school-wide ticket is going to be used, we recommend using Effective Praise to reinforce the desired behavior and giving the student a reason for continuing the behavior in the future that ties it to positive outcome. The following graphic represents how the strategies of reinforcement can be used as a multi-tiered system of support in the Well-Managed Schools program.

Universal Interventions

- Reinforce appropriate student behavior using primarily general and specific praise.

- Strive for a 4:1 praise-to-correction ratio.

- Increase specificity for new or difficult behaviors/skills.

- Reinforce students as soon as possible.

- Use generalized Effective Praise to reinforce developing skills for the whole class.

Secondary Interventions

- Use specific praise with greater frequency.

- Use skill-focused Effective Praise for new/difficult skills.

- Reinforce approximations of appropriate behaviors.

Tertiary Interventions

- Maintain a minimum of a 4:1 praise-to-correction ratio.

- Use frequent, skill-focused Effective Praise for targeted skills.

- Reinforce approximations of appropriate behaviors.

- Collaborate with outside resources to provide additional positive support.

- Use Effective Praise combined with positive consequences or within a motivation system.

Final Thoughts

We began this chapter by quoting an educator who didn't believe in the value or relevance of praising students. Praise, like many of the other preventive strategies outlined in Section II, is sometimes viewed with much skepticism or little enthusiasm. We want to conclude this chapter with thoughts from a different teacher, one who learned that praise as a component in a larger classroom management strategy is an effective tool for change:

"What can someone from Nebraska tell me about discipline in my classroom? You don't know my kids or their problems. It's not going to work." This middle school teacher in a large, urban East Coast school district was resistant to implementing any of the classroom management strategies we advocated, including praise. A few months into the school year, however, the teacher's voice had worn out. When Fridays rolled around, her voice was hoarse and faint from yelling so often during the week to discipline unruly students. Frustrated by her now-chronic vocal condition and the lack of any meaningful improvement in student behavior, she confided to us, "This is not me. This is not the kind of classroom I want to have."

The teacher realized she had to do something different. She began incorporating into her school day several Well-Managed School methods, including using empathy statements, rationales (both of these strategies and others that are used to correct problem behaviors will be examined in Chapter 13), and praise. She approached discipline issues from a more proactive, rather than reactive, perspective and positive change soon followed. In a matter of weeks, she not only found her voice (because she wasn't yelling at her students as much), but also saw an increase in in-class instruction time (Burke, Guck, Robinson, Powell, & O'Neil Fichtner, 2006). Sometimes, one's own resistance to change and adopting new strategies in the classroom proves to be the greatest obstacle to overcome.

This teacher's use of praise was not the sole reason her students' behavior improved. As a single intervention strategy, praise is unlikely to produce the long-term benefits and outcomes you desire. However, this teacher's experience shows us that in a comprehensive classroom management program, the use of praise should not be excluded nor its potential discounted.

Correcting Problem Behaviors

Devon enters your classroom with his head down and his stride slow. You look at him and say, "Good afternoon, Devon." He responds by dropping his head even lower and walking faster to his desk. He says nothing.

You're disappointed by his behavior. Devon doesn't usually greet people, but it's a skill you've been working on with him for the past several weeks. You wonder if something happened to Devon in the hallway or earlier in the day that may have upset him. You approach him at his desk and ask, "Devon, why didn't you greet me when you came into class?"

He looks straight ahead and tersely mumbles, "Cause I don't feel like talking to you!"

How do you respond? Will you:

- Walk away.

- Ask him softly, "Why don't you feel like talking to me today?"

- Tell him sternly, "I expect you to greet me whenever you enter my classroom."

- Pat him on the shoulder and say, "That's okay."

- Laugh it off and tell him he'll be happier when the class period is over.

- Roll your eyes, mutter "Typical," and ignore him for the rest of the period.

This situation, like any difficult or less-than-pleasant interaction with students, illustrates the many behavioral choices you have when responding to problem behaviors. How you choose to react can determine whether or not a situation or behavior improves, worsens, or simply never changes. In this chapter, we examine strategies to successfully correct problem behaviors, including how to manage your own actions and attitudes so you are a positive agent for change rather than an obstacle.

The Conflict Cycle

If you react to Devon by rolling your eyes and turning your back on him, you simply mirror the same disrespectful behaviors he demonstrated. Now Devon might feel you "dissed" him, and become even more defiant. Suddenly, what began as a seemingly innocuous incident escalates into an all-out, in-your-face confrontation. This back and forth, or action-reaction cycle, is a process that researchers Nicholas Long and Mary Wood refer to as the Conflict Cycle, and it goes on every day in classrooms and schools across the country.

According to Long and Wood (1990), crisis is the product of a child's (or student's) stress that is kept alive by the actions and reactions of others. When a child's feelings are aroused by stress, he or she learns to behave in ways that shield him or her from painful feelings. These behaviors are inappropriate, but they protect the youth from undesirable, distressing feelings. Others (parents, teachers, peers) perceive the behavior as negative, and they respond in a negative fashion toward the youth. This negative response produces additional stress and the youth again reacts in an inappropriate manner. This spiraling of behaviors causes a minor incident to escalate into a crisis.

The Conflict Cycle follows a predictable pattern: First, there is a stressful event (failing an exam, getting rejected by peers, etc.) that triggers an irrational or negative belief ("The teacher is out to get me!" or "Everyone in school hates me!"). These negative thoughts trigger negative feelings and anxieties, which drive inappropriate behavior. The inappropriate behavior (talking back, cursing, being sarcastic, etc.) provokes others who then mirror those negative behaviors. Their adverse reaction increases a student's stress, triggers more intense feelings, and drives more negative behavior. The student's behavior leads to even more anger and frustration on the part of those around him or her. This cycle continues until it escalates into a no-win power struggle (Long, Wood, & Fecser, 2001).

For most teachers, the biggest challenge to correcting inappropriate behavior is staying out of or breaking the Conflict Cycle. When a student yells, "I'm not going to do this crap!", the natural urge is to yell right back, "Oh, yes you will!" But matching the student's actions or escalating your behaviors in response to the student's inappropriate actions only starts the cycle spinning. Then, the goal becomes winning the argument rather than teaching an alternative behavior or correcting the problem. It's a lose-lose proposition. Avoiding the natural instinct to act aggressively when faced with an aggressive student, however, can be difficult.

Long (1995) identified seven reasons or circumstances that trigger acts of "counteraggression" from adults. Answering aggression with aggression is most likely to happen if adults:

Conflict Cycle
(Long, Wood, & Fecser, 2001)

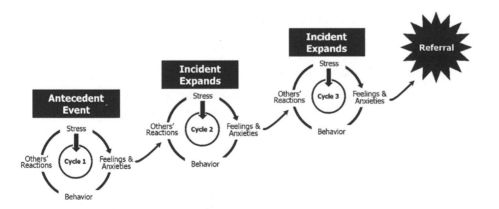

1. **Get caught up in the Conflict Cycle.**

   The Conflict Cycle accounts for as much as 50 percent of counteraggressive actions. When a teacher or staff member mirrors the inappropriate behavior of a student, the situation becomes "more emotional, irrational, and volatile" (p. 12).

2. **Believe their personal and cherished values and beliefs are being violated.**

   When a student violates or opposes a value or virtue that a teacher holds dear – being polite, prompt, honest, etc. – it can elicit strong emotions from the teacher, which can turn into aggressive responses.

3. **Are in a bad mood.**

   There are days when people are simply discouraged or upset. Family problems, financial strains, job stress, failed relationships, or some life issue has them down in the dumps. When a teacher has a bad day, any behavioral mistake from a student can unleash an avalanche of emotions.

4. **Feel as if they are not meeting professional expectations.**

   This happens when teachers, despite what their training and experience tells them, allow questionable or potentially explosive situations to happen or continue. When things blow up, the teachers are mad at themselves for letting it happen, but direct their anger at the students.

5. **Feel rejected and helpless.**

   When a teacher believes he or she has a special bond or connection with a struggling student, the teacher willingly goes above and beyond to help that student succeed. But when the relationship deteriorates because the student makes unrealistic demands, refuses to listen, or pulls away for whatever reason, the teacher feels exploited or manipulated. Feeling slighted after all he or she has done, the teacher reacts by rejecting the student.

6. **Prejudge a student in crisis.**

   Some students have reputations that precede them, for better or worse. When a student known for his or her behavioral problems is in the middle of a chaotic situation, it's often assumed he or she is the cause. If a teacher accuses an innocent student before knowing all the facts, the student gets upset, the teacher assumes the student is lying, and chaos turns into crisis.

7. **Have unfinished or unresolved psychological issues.**

   Teachers bring their life experiences into the classroom. Those experiences affect how they see themselves, their students, and their students' behaviors. For example, if a teacher was the victim of severe bullying as a child, he or she may be particularly sensitive to harassment and discrimination. Seeing someone verbally or physically beat up another student may trigger feelings of rage as the teacher recalls his or her own past. The teacher's impulse is to bully the bully.

As you can see, getting caught up in a cycle of "tit-for-tat" behaviors can happen when psychological, biological, and emotional issues get the best of you. With so many factors potentially influencing actions and reactions, there is only one thing that is certain: You have the power to control your own behavior. The better able you are to stay calm, maintain your professional demeanor, and remember that students' behavioral mistakes are really teaching opportunities, the better and more effective your response to difficult situations and behaviors will be.

How you maintain a professional demeanor (demonstrating the quality components referred to in Chapter 12) can involve everything from your voice tone to word choice. Using a soft but firm voice is less inflammatory than using a raised or sarcastic tone. It also helps if you speak in a controlled manner – slow and calm – rather than fast and overly emotional. Keeping a relaxed posture and using non-aggressive body language can also defuse escalating tensions. A non-aggressive stance means you aren't doing things like raising a fist at the student, pointing in his or her face, violating the student's personal space by towering over him or her, or using any other gesture that could provoke a hostile reaction. Perhaps most importantly, avoid making judgmental statements. Don't attack the student personally or make belittling or disparaging statements about him or her. Keep your comments brief and focused on the inappropriate behavior rather than arguing about who's at fault or bringing up other content unrelated to the actual behavior.

Another key to avoiding the Conflict Cycle is being aware of your emotional hot buttons. What can a student say or do to send you shooting straight over the edge? If certain behaviors drive you crazy (because your tolerance level for that behavior is especially low), prepare for those situations by practicing self-control strategies that calm your nerves – deep breathing, counting to 10, positive self-talk, etc. When you feel your frustration rising and your emotions starting to dictate your responses, don't hesitate to step back and regain your composure. You might consider turning your attention to another student who needs academic help or looking for any positive behaviors shown by others in the class. When it comes to correcting a student's behavior, success starts with your own actions.

Managing the Environment

Just as your behavior can influence the frequency and severity of problem behaviors, so too can the environment. Later, we'll examine specific strategies and responses for dealing with and correcting inappropriate behavior. But in order for those strategies to work successfully, you first have to cultivate a climate or culture that defines behavioral expectations and allows values such as respect, responsibility, and accountability to flourish.

We've already discussed numerous elements that need to be in place to create a positive classroom and school; for example, the need for and significance of establishing rules and procedures (Chapters 6 and 7). Both offer students structure and reinforce behavioral expectations. Also, the use of praise (Chapter 12) acknowledges students' successes and reaffirms their progress. Praise is also a behavioral motivator and helps build and sustain positive relationships with students. Likewise, negative consequences (Chapter 8) remind students that poor choices come with a cost and should be avoided. And preventive social skills instruction (Chapter 11) empowers students with the ability to think differently, act differently, and make better decisions. All of these measures, when used consistently and collaboratively, help to deter inattentive, disruptive, and undisciplined behaviors. They are not, however, a panacea for poor behavior. Problems will flare up. Still, it's much easier to deal with inappropriate behavior when students are already immersed in a culture that teaches, promotes, supports, and values good behavior. In such an environment, your efforts to correct a problem situation are supported because the environment itself reinforces everything you teach. At the end of this chapter, we'll examine another aspect of managing the environment – neutralizing or containing a problem situation so it doesn't ensnare more students.

Managing Yourself and Behavioral Learning

Having looked at how your actions can influence students' behaviors and how the environment either reinforces or works against your efforts to correct students, we can now discuss the actual teaching strategies for correcting inappropriate behavior when it happens.

The strategy you use to address inappropriate behavior will depend largely on the magnitude of what's going on. Intervening or correcting two students involved in a brawl requires a different response than dealing with two students caught passing notes. Just as inappropriate behaviors fall on a continuum of severity, intervention strategies can also be viewed on a continuum of restrictiveness, from least (modeling behavior, giving corrective prompts, etc.) to most (full-blown teaching interactions that include giving negative consequences, office referrals, etc.). Ideally, you'll want to use the least-restrictive intervention that will motivate students to turn their behavior around, allowing them to remain in class, and is appropriate for the circumstances. In other words, sending a student to the office for a first-time, minor offense (talking during class, passing notes, failing to greet you properly, etc.) may be quick and convenient for you, but it's an overreaction that wastes the administrator's time, denies the student valuable in-class instruction, and may generate harsh feelings (at best) or hostile responses (at worst) from the student. This kind of punitive reaction is especially troubling and unnecessary when subtler and more constructive responses can achieve the desired goal – getting the student back on task and in control of his or her behavior.

CHOOSING INTERVENTIONS

Ideally, you'll want to use the least restrictive intervention that will motivate students to turn their behavior around, allowing them to remain in class, and is appropriate given the circumstances.

Demanding a "pound of flesh" (wanting to be vengeful and punishing, rather than constructive and teaching), regardless of how minor the infraction is, is unfortunate and ineffective. But the opposite response isn't much better. Ignoring or overlooking problem behaviors is often what leads to bigger, more emotionally intense situations. Teachers and administrators in the best-run schools and best-managed classrooms put their efforts and energies into preventing students from becoming emotionally intense or out of control. But too often, some educators seem more interested in knowing how to stop a student who is tossing books, overturning desks, cursing, or fighting than in learning what can be done to prevent such outbursts in the first place. Doing the little things so big things don't happen is what we call "managing the learning." This approach consists of strategies that correct problem behaviors by teaching students better alternatives without antagonizing them or pushing them toward even more aggressive actions.

These strategies can help you to shape and promote student self-control:

Modeling – As the Conflict Cycle so pointedly demonstrates, the most powerful tool at your disposal is your ability to model the behavior you want to see from your students. Most teachers are great at modeling academic behaviors. For example, a math teacher will explain an algebraic formula step-by-step and give students practice problems so they can apply the formula in true-to-life situations. For a spelling lesson, a teacher will go over a word list, have students practice by spelling words aloud or writing them down, and create flash cards to help facilitate learning. Modeling academic behaviors is simply showing students what to do to help them learn a subject. When it comes to social behaviors, you have to be just as diligent and specific about modeling what you want students to do in your classroom and school.

Let's go back to Devon, who we introduced at the beginning of the chapter. Greeting students and having them greet you is a skill or component of the school day that some deem important and necessary. This skill is a relatively easy way to start making a positive difference in the overall climate of a school. A simple greeting sets a positive tone, creates a welcoming, warm situation, and develops or reinforces more connected relationships between teachers and students. For these reasons, it's worthwhile to blend this element into the school day, regardless of the setting or grade level. With Devon or any student, it's important for you to model the kind of friendly greeting you would like to see on a daily basis, no matter how the student enters your classroom. Smiling, making eye contact, saying the student's name, and using an upbeat voice tone are behaviors you should model.

It's counterproductive to mirror, or mock, any poor behaviors a student might demonstrate: mumbling a response because the student mumbled, hanging your head down because the student didn't make eye contact, or completely ignoring a student whose greeting isn't "perfect."

Corrective prompts – You already use corrective prompts, though you may not realize it. For example, if two students whisper back and forth during your lecture, you might look at them and put your finger over your mouth, or you might walk closer to their desks. These nonverbal prompts tell the students to be quiet. Or, you may prompt them by verbally stating their names. Maybe you have "the look," which many teachers have. It's a facial expression that tells students they need to stop whatever they're doing or face a more severe consequence. For some students, a corrective prompt is all that's needed to get them to change their behavior or recall a skill you want them to use. Here is how a corrective prompt might look and sound with Devon if he walks past the teacher without offering a greeting:

> **Teacher:** Smiles, and in a positive voice, says, "Hey Devon, where's my greeting?"
>
> **Devon:** "Oh yeah. Sorry, I forgot. Good morning Ms. Dillon."

Corrective strategies – This is a group of five separate responses that offer more specificity than a corrective prompt. These strategies give students time to reflect on their situation and give teachers additional strategies for their tool belt. They are also useful when trying to calm a young person. The five corrective strategies are:

MANAGING YOURSELF MEANS…

- Using a soft voice tone.
- Being aware of body language.
- Maintaining safe proximity.
- Using a slow rate of speech/pacing.
- Continuing to use corrective strategies (cool-down time, coupling statements, reality statements/reasons, empathy, and specific praise).
- Allowing cool-down time.
- Staying away from content (focus on behavior, not motives or blame).

---

1. **Cool-down time** – This can help you as much as the student. With this strategy, you give the student a specific length of time and a task that will help him or her reflect on and think about how to turn a behavior around. You're not forcing a conversation. This is time you also can use to calm yourself or to make sure other students are doing what they need to do so they don't involve themselves in the situation. With Devon, cool-down time might look and sound something like this:

   Teacher: Stands in classroom entrance and says, "Hi, Devon."

   Devon: Walks by and sarcastically replies, "I don't feel like saying 'Hi' today."

   Teacher: Walks to Devon's desk, squats, and says, "I tell you what, Devon. I'm going to give you a couple of minutes to get your notebook out and prepare for class while I answer a few questions. When I'm done, I'll come back and we'll talk about that greeting."

2. **Coupling statements** – These are brief statements in which you describe a student's inappropriate behavior while offering a more appropriate alternative behavior. This concept was discussed earlier in Chapter 4, "Observing and Describing Behavior." Coupling statements are effective if you avoid vague or judgmental terms and keep your descriptions specific. Avoid overusing any one particular phrase, especially those that may set off a power struggle, such as "You need to…" or "I want you to…." Perhaps the most important function of a coupling statement is that it serves as a check on your emotions. In other words, if you focus primarily on observing and describing the student's behavior, you are less likely to react emotionally, thereby worsening the situation. Here is an example of a coupling statement that could be used with Devon, followed by one that is ineffective because it lacks specificity.

   Specific
   Teacher: "Devon, you walked into class with your head down and said nothing. A better choice would be to look up and greet me with a 'Hi' or 'Hello.'"

Nonspecific
Teacher: "You're acting glum. Cheer up."

Many times, a student will be engaging in several inappropriate behaviors. In these situations, it's important to describe the most overt or intrusive behavior. For example, if Devon came into class glaring at you, waving his arms, and arguing in a loud voice, the behavior you should address is the arguing. Loud arguing is probably the most disruptive behavior, and it would be difficult to do any further teaching until it diminishes or stops. A coupling statement in this case might sound like this: "Instead of arguing, Devon, please be quiet."

3. **Reality statements/reasons** – Always make sure you provide students with the "why" of engaging in certain behaviors. Reality statements and reasons (rationales) are ways to communicate the "why" to students. Both can point out potential benefits or negative outcomes. With rationales (discussed in Chapter 5), students are more likely to understand the benefits of following your instructions and accepting the merits of your teaching. By highlighting the potential outcomes (what is likely to happen) of using a skill or regaining self-control, students can make better choices about their behavior. Reality statements are similar to reasons, but they point out something that's real and relevant to the student's immediate situation rather than something that might happen. Here are a few examples:

A reality statement with Devon that points out a negative outcome might sound like this:

Teacher: "Devon, we're going to work in lab today, and no one wants to work with you when you don't look at them, talk to them, or act friendly toward them."

A reality statement that highlights a positive outcome might sound like this:

Teacher: "Devon, when you greet me and other students in class, you get started off on the right foot by setting a positive tone, and it shows you're ready to get started."

A reason or rationale that points out a negative outcome might sound like this:

Teacher: "Devon, if you ignore someone's greeting or don't offer your own, you appear unfriendly and that can hurt your chances of making new friends."

A reason or rationale that points out a positive outcome might sound like this:

Teacher: "Devon, by greeting someone appropriately, you can develop a reputation as someone who is polite and friendly."

4. **Empathy** – This strategy is particularly appropriate and effective when you have a student who is struggling with a skill. Sometimes, when students have repeated difficulties with a behavior or skill, it turns into an excuse to not try anymore. You must convince students not to give up. A statement that lets a student know you understand his or her situation or experiences can help de-escalate a problem behavior. For example, if Devon is an introvert and greeting people is naturally difficult for him, correcting him on his inappropriate greeting might begin with a statement like this:

    Teacher: "Devon, I know it's really tough greeting people. Even I struggle with it sometimes because I have a shy personality. But try your best. It gets easier the more you do it."

5. **Specific praise** – Reinforcing students when they make good choices is as important as correcting them when they make a mistake. When correcting a problem behavior, acknowledge any appropriate responses or actions the student takes. Recognizing any effort the student makes and reinforcing behavioral approximations (doing some of the steps to a skill or positive behavior) can help the student regain self-control and maintain appropriate behaviors. By praising the prosocial behaviors, you increase the likelihood that these behaviors will continue or be used more frequently. In Devon's case, if he doesn't greet you but manages to get to class quietly and on time (normally he's loud and late), use specific praise to reinforce those positive steps. (Acknowledging small improvements is an example of behavioral shaping, which we

discussed in Chapter 3.). A specific praise statement might sound like this:

Teacher: "Devon, thank you for getting to class before the bell rang and talking quietly when you entered. Why don't you go ahead and give me a greeting like we've been practicing?"

Guided self-correction – This is a problem-solving process you can use with a student when he or she is agreeable and willing to have a conversation with you. When a student is too upset to listen or argues and becomes aggravated, more intensive strategies (discussed in Chapter 14) may be necessary. For guided self-correction to be effective, the student has to understand that he or she made a mistake and knows how to correct it, and be willing to talk with you about what happened. Guided-self correction is essentially a conversation that helps the student analyze and learn from the mistake. This is what guided self-correction might sound like with Devon:

Step 1: Acknowledge the behavior or situation, assuming the student is willing to talk.

Teacher: "Let's talk about what just happened."

Step 2: Ask the student what he or she did.

Teacher: "Devon, what did you do when I greeted you?"

Devon: "When I came in, I rushed past you and didn't say 'Hello.'"

Step 3: Ask the student what he or she should have done.

Teacher: "Yes, you did. Thanks for being honest. Can you tell me what you should have done to greet me appropriately?"

Devon: "I guess I should have stopped, made eye contact, and said, 'Hi' or 'Hello.'"

Step 4: Ask the student to give you a rationale for using the skill appropriately.

Teacher: "Absolutely! Why is it important to greet me that way?"

Devon: "Because it shows you I'm ready for class, and I'm in a good mood."

Step 5.: Ask the student how he or she can improve on a skill.

Teacher: "Okay. So, how are you going to greet me next time?"

Devon: "When I come in tomorrow, I'm going to make sure I stop, look at you, and say 'Hi' or 'Hello.'"

Teacher: "Sounds good. I'll be watching."

Corrective Teaching

The fifth strategy for shaping and promoting behavioral change in students is Corrective Teaching. This approach is more restrictive and requires more in-depth teaching than the previous four strategies. Typically, you will try to motivate behavior change using a prompt or other corrective strategy before moving on to Corrective Teaching. It would be impossible, as well as unnecessary, to do Corrective Teaching in response to every inappropriate behavior. However, when the previously discussed strategies do not diminish or stop a behavior, Corrective Teaching is the next option.

Corrective Teaching combines many of the methods discussed earlier in this chapter and book – praise, descriptions of the inappropriate behavior and the appropriate alternative behavior, rationales, practice, and consequences. This higher level of individualized instruction becomes necessary when a student's behavior is severe enough (swearing at you or other students, etc.) or repeated often enough (always talking out of turn, etc.) that it demands greater attention. The extra time and effort involved with this strategy is aimed at empowering a student to make better choices rather than simply trying to suppress his or her problem behaviors.

There are six components, or steps, to Corrective Teaching. Consistently using this strategy in an atmosphere of genuine concern for students will, over time, help them learn better responses to potential problems.

The Corrective Teaching steps are:

1. **Offer initial praise or empathy.**

2. **Describe the inappropriate behavior.**

3. **Describe the appropriate behavior.**

4. **Give a rationale.**

5. **Practice.**

6. **Use a negative consequence (optional).**

1. **Offer initial praise or empathy** – One way to begin your interaction is with a positive statement related to the behavior you are teaching. Your praise will sound more genuine if it relates to the teaching situation. For example, Shonda wants your attention. She waves her arm in the air and calls out loudly, "Hey, I need some help over here!" What is praiseworthy about that? There are a number of behaviors you could recognize: staying in her seat, raising her hand, asking for help, staying on task, and making eye contact. Going back to our example with Devon, when you greet him, he rushes past you and says nothing. Although it appears Devon didn't do anything to warrant praise, you could acknowledge the fact that he made it to class on time and went straight to his desk, or maybe that, on the way, he picked up a pen dropped by a classmate. More often than not, a student does something, be it ever so modest, that can be acknowledged and praised.

   Initial praise reinforces approximations of the desired behavior and helps students recognize their progress. It enhances your relationships with students by showing them that you are aware of their accomplishments, even when they display inappropriate behaviors. Also, by focusing on something a student did well, you start the interaction on a positive note and are less likely to be seen as antagonizing or punishing.

   You might also choose to start your interaction with an empathy statement to let the student know you understand what he or she is experiencing. Like praise, empathy helps set a positive tone and makes students more receptive to your correction. Using Shonda's situation as an example, you may empathize with her needing help by saying, "I can understand you'd really like some help with your assignment." Often, older students respond better to empathy than praise because it sounds more genuine and less contrived.

Without the consistent use of this initial step, students may see you as punishing – someone who is quick to criticize mistakes and slow to recognize accomplishments. If this happens, students might actively try to avoid you or immediately escalate their behaviors because you represent negative consequences to them.

2. **Describe the inappropriate behavior** – This step involves describing, in specific terms, the student's inappropriate behavior. Using objective, behavioral terms, describe the antecedent events that led up to the behavior and the student's actions in order to structure your teaching. With Devon, for example, you might say: "When you came in this afternoon and I said 'Hello,' you did not look at me and rushed past without saying anything." This description "sets the stage" for your teaching by providing the student with a clear picture of what he did, and helping you decide what skill to teach.

    Avoid using judgmental terms in your conversation. Describe the behaviors instead of their perceived intent or motive. For example, instead of asking a student, "Why are you being so mean to Ashanti? You're just trying to make her cry, aren't you?", focus on the specific behavior. A more effective statement is, "When you passed by Ashanti's desk, you called her a derogatory name and then laughed at her."

    Using brief, to-the-point descriptions can prevent you from badgering the student or having the student perceive your teaching as badgering. Point out the most overt or obvious behavior, then move on. The purpose of this step is to increase the student's awareness of the behavior so you can shift the emphasis to providing him or her with more appropriate alternatives. Also, if the student acts inattentive or distracted at any point during Corrective Teaching, give him or her a prompt to pay attention. For example, you could say: "Logan, could you put your book down and look at me, please?" Sometimes, the student's inattentive or disruptive behavior will continue, escalate, or reoccur frequently. Strategies for dealing with these more emotionally intense situations are discussed in the next chapter.

3. **Describe the appropriate behavior** – After you've described the problem behavior, it's time to teach the student an appropriate alternative. By doing this, you not only help the student understand your expectations, but also assist him or her in learning social skills that can be used in other settings. To promote this generalization, use words like, "Devon, a better way to greet someone…" or "Whenever someone gives you feedback…." This phrasing, rather than "I" statements, such as "I'd like you to…," focuses the student on using self-management skills instead of teacher-pleasing behaviors.

   As part of your description, label the skill you are teaching so it is clear for you and the student. Teach each of the incremental behaviors that comprise the skill. With Devon, you might say: "Devon, a better way to greet people is to look at them, smile, use a pleasant tone of voice, and say something like, 'Good morning.'" If necessary, you can demonstrate or model the behaviors in order to make the description clear for the student.

4. **Give a rationale** – Offering the student a rationale after describing the appropriate behavior tells him or her why the skill should be learned and used. The rationale should be personal, skill-based, and brief, and explain the short-term benefits the student can receive by using the skill. This helps the student internalize the behavior. In addition to explaining the benefits of using a skill, your rationale also might point out negative outcomes for not using the skill or how the student's behavior affects others. Rationales also empower students to understand that their behavioral choices, in part, determine what may happen to them. For a review of the types and benefits of rationales and a more in-depth discussion, refer to Chapter 5, "Providing Reasons: How to Link Behavior to Results."

5. **Practice** – Having a student practice an alternative positive behavior provides him or her with an opportunity to immediately use the skill in a "low-risk" situation. Just as practice helps a student learn an academic concept, the practice step acts as a bridge between the initial inappropriate behavior and progress toward mastering an alternative social skill.

The student's performance during the practice also gives you an idea of how well you taught the skill. This is the only time during Corrective Teaching where you can assess your instructional effectiveness and determine whether reteaching is necessary.

In order for the practice to be truly effective, you have to set it up very clearly for the student. The student should know exactly what he or she is supposed to do, what skill is being practiced, and what you are going to do. For example, in setting up a practice on how to greet someone, you might say: "Devon, here's an opportunity to use greeting skills just like we talked about. This time, you'll look at me, smile, and in a pleasant voice tone say, 'Good afternoon.'" After explaining what you want the student to do, ask if he or she understands. You might say something like, "Does that make sense?" Then give the student a cue to begin the practice so you separate your set-up from the actual role-play.

(It's important to note that you can set up practice situations without asking a student if he or she wants to practice. Depending on the student, such a question may generate any number of inappropriate replies. Also, older adolescents sometimes can be put off by the word "practice." You may want to use phrases like "Let's try again" or "How about a do over?" instead.)

Usually, you will have the student practice the skill in the original context. In other words, if the student had trouble accepting criticism about a term paper, you'd give him or her the same criticism in practice. If the original interaction was somewhat "heated," make sure you prompt the student that you're going to practice the same situation again. This may help you avoid any of the difficulties the student had with the original situation and bring closure to the episode.

Practice sessions can sometimes be more successful and helpful to the student if you use a similar but hypothetical situation. This is especially true if the original issue involved a very emotional or intense response by the student, or if it was disruptive to your class. Under these circumstances, you should teach the skill in a different context. For example,

Nicholas is out of his seat looking out the window. You give him an instruction to sit down, but he remains standing for quite some time before going back to his desk. Now, when you teach the skill of "Following Instructions," it would distract the class and Nicholas if you sent him back to the window during the practice. So, a better option would be to have him practice following another instruction, such as getting started on his assignment, opening his book to a specific page, or taking out necessary supplies for the class. All of these instructions would lead Nicholas toward getting back on task with the rest of the class. Similarly, if the original situation involved an intense reaction by the student, you might practice the skill in a pretend situation first. If the practice goes well, you could role-play the skill again in the context of the actual event.

Sometimes, the practice step of Corrective Teaching should be done later, at a more suitable time. For example, a student who comes into class late may have to practice being on time when she goes to her next class or when she returns to your class the next day. Or, a student may need to see you after school to finish getting your feedback and help on an assignment, and you could review and practice accepting feedback then, if no in-class time is available.

In any practice situation, if the student doesn't achieve predetermined criteria, he or she should practice again. Most of the time, the student will practice the skill as you described it. However, for students who are just learning skills, you may have to be satisfied if they can demonstrate some or most of the behavioral steps of the skill. These students are in the "shaping" process; they need to be praised for approximating desired behaviors. With time and effort, mastery will come.

6. **Use a negative consequence (response cost and positive correction)** – Giving a consequence is an optional step because sometimes just having a conversation with students and having them practice the skill is enough to change behavior. For some students, the embarrassment or disappointment of being corrected provides enough motivation to get them back on task and stay on task. For others, engaging in inappropriate behavior demands a more tangible negative

consequence (response cost). In other words, the student loses something that is reinforcing to him or her. The purpose of a negative consequence is to deter the student from engaging in that behavior again.

When giving a negative consequence, consideration should be given to the following:

Size of the consequence. How large does the consequence have to be in order to be effective? It's best to start small, using the least amount of response cost possible to produce the desired change. When deciding the size of the consequence, consider the frequency with which the behavior occurs and its severity. A frequent or severe behavior should warrant a larger or more punitive consequence. For example, will keeping the student after school to practice a skill be enough to change his or her behavior, or should you make a phone call home?

Difficulty of the desired behavior or skill. Consider how difficult it is for the student to perform the appropriate behavior. If the student is very deficient in the skill of "Following Instructions," for example, he or she will probably need many opportunities to practice the skill during the course of the school day, and many practices will involve mistakes. If you were to give a large consequence every time the student didn't follow instructions, he or she would quickly get buried in penalties by mid-morning, feel frustrated and angry, and have little incentive to work on using the skill.

Appropriateness of the consequence. Just like with rewards, negative consequences need to be individualized to ensure that they are indeed effective. You can determine the effectiveness of a response cost by looking at the behavioral outcome. If the behavior diminishes or disappears, the consequence was effective. If the behavior continues or intensifies, it was not. Here's an example: Sanjay loves playing soccer with his friends at recess. When he has trouble staying on task during class, he loses 10 minutes of his recess so he can practice the skill and finish his assignments. Losing those 10 minutes of soccer time is enough of a consequence to help Sanjay stay on task the rest of the day and the following day. However, if Sanjay usually plays by himself or hangs out with you during recess, losing these 10 minutes won't matter. A better consequence might be sending a note home to his parents.

Consequences should be viewed on a continuum. At one end is the least punitive consequence that will promote the greatest desired behavior change. On the other end is the largest or most severe consequence that would potentially bring about a change in a student's behavior.

Even when you do not give a consequence as part of a Corrective Teaching interaction, the interaction itself serves as a consequence. The student must pay attention, listen, and spend time with you to practice a skill or appropriate alternative behavior. Pointing this consequence out helps him or her understand there was a consequence. Using Devon again as an example, Corrective Teaching as a consequence could end something like this: "Because you had trouble greeting me this afternoon, we had to take a few extra minutes to discuss a better way to greet people and practice the skill. But you did a nice practice, so why don't you take your seat and we'll get started on the assignment." The Corrective Teaching interaction by itself can be significant enough that no additional consequences need to be given.

Many students have difficulty seeing the connection between their behavior and the consequences that follow. Therefore, it's a good idea to point out to students what other logical consequences (besides the Corrective Teaching interaction) can happen as a result of their inappropriate behavior. For example, during class, Daryl yells out, "Hey, I don't understand this question!" At the same time, another student raises her hand for help. Because the second student is seeking help appropriately, you go to her first. Then you go to Daryl. Before you answer his question, you correct him for his inappropriate outburst and have him practice a more appropriate way to get your attention. As a result, Daryl doesn't get the help he needs as quickly as he wanted and can't move on to the next question. You can point out this consequence by saying something like, "Because you had a hard time getting my attention appropriately, it took you longer to get the clarification you needed. Now that we've discussed what happened, we can work on answering your question."

When students practice a skill sincerely, regain their composure, or accept a consequence without complaint, it's a good idea to recognize their efforts with positive correction. Essentially, positive correction is a small reward that scales back or takes away some of the negative consequence. Whether you use positive correction is dependent on how well the student practices the skill with you and responds to the other components of Corrective Teaching. For example, Keilani was repeatedly off task and didn't complete her assignment. Because she didn't get her work done, she earned 30 minutes of detention with you. After school, Keilani talks to you about her behavior and what she should have done differently. During detention, she practices how to stay on task by finishing her assignment in 20 minutes. Because she accepted her consequence without arguing or getting upset, acknowledged her mistake, and practiced the skill, you tell her she earned the privilege of leaving detention 10 minutes early. For some students, knowing they might be able to earn back some of what they lost gives them hope and motivates them to change their behavior. This is especially true for students who feel so buried under a negative consequence, they see no point in trying anymore.

One last consideration regarding consequences is that some situations demand compensatory behavior and/or restitution, which is another logical outcome. For example, if Bo starts a fight with a classmate, you can have him apologize for his actions and do something nice for the other student as part of his consequence. Or if Bo defaces a mural, his consequence might be to help clean off the graffiti and repaint the mural. If a problem behavior is too severe or becomes habitual, it may be a good idea to have a conference with the parents or guardians to discuss other intervention options.

As we've said throughout this chapter, when you correct students' inappropriate behaviors, it's imperative that you are conscious of your own actions. Even though your focus is on correcting a behavioral mistake, you must concentrate on conveying care and concern. The warmth and genuineness (or lack thereof) of your interaction is revealed through your general tone and behavior. You can make your teaching more pleasant with what we call "quality components," such as looking at the student, having a relaxed posture, using a pleasant voice tone, calling the student by name, and having a pleasant or neutral facial expression. Maintaining these behaviors throughout Corrective Teaching helps personalize your instruction and demonstrates your respect for the student and his or her dignity. As a result, the student will be more receptive to your feedback, and you can maintain a positive tone.

The ultimate goal of using Corrective Teaching is to give your students a cognitive tool for self-management. Initially, you guide your students through each step and help them identify more appropriate behaviors. Eventually, they will incorporate what you have taught and be empowered to correct their social errors independently.

Limiting the Effects of Misbehaviors

Whatever your response – modeling, corrective prompts, corrective strategies, guided self-correction, or Corrective Teaching – to a problem behavior, keep in mind that you're not working with one student in total isolation. Other young people or an entire class of students will be part of the mix. Earlier in the chapter, we examined how to manage the environment in terms of being proactive and implementing strategies to diminish the potential for disruptions or complete chaos. But part of managing the environment also involves containing situations that do develop and limiting their effects on others.

First, there may be times when a student's behavior is so outrageous or blatant (swearing in elementary school or fighting in high school) that school policy requires an automatic office referral. If the behavior is borderline, you'll have to make a judgment call on whether an office referral is better than using a less-restrictive method of intervention. As part of your deliberation, and managing the environment, you have to ask yourself if the other students in the classroom or area are safe. If you feel they are not, then send the disruptive student to the office. If he or she refuses or lingers, then get help from other staff or the school resource officer. If necessary, have the other students go into the hallway, library, or another safe place until the disruptive student is a little calmer. (We'll talk more about de-escalations in the next chapter.)

Hopefully, such extreme situations will be infrequent. But you should have a plan in place for managing everyone else while you deal with an individual student for an extended period of time, or if you have to turn your attention away from the class for any reason. Keeping students on task when other things are happening around them is part of managing the environment. In Chapter 7, we introduced the concept of DEAR Time (Drop Everything And Read). This is a prompt you can use while taking care of an issue or behavior problem that interrupts your teaching. Its purpose is to keep students occupied with a specific task instead of doing whatever they want – talking, moving around the room, etc. Teach this kind of prompt proactively and periodically to students, preferably at times that are not stressful. Similar concepts educators use include Independent Time and MYOB – Mind Your Own Behavior. Again, these are prompts that tell students what to do while you focus on something other than teaching them at that moment. For example, you might teach students to do the following when they hear you say "Independent Time": Keep your head and face forward, keep your eyes on the paper in front of you, work on the assignment you're given, and stay silent. Having this kind of plan in place when a student becomes disruptive or your lesson plan is interrupted helps manage other students' behaviors and brings more calm and control to the situation.

MISTAKES ARE TEACHING OPPORTUNITIES

You have the power to control your own behavior. The better able you are to stay calm, maintain your professional demeanor, and remember that students' behavioral mistakes are really teaching opportunities, the better and more effective your response to difficult situations and behaviors will be.

Multi-Tiered Systems of Support

Correction is a continuum of strategies teachers can use to redirect and manage student behavior. It is important that teachers have a large toolbox when managing student behavior so they can maintain self-control and model the behavior they would like to see. No matter what strategy you end up using, you have to determine if it was effective by measuring whether the intensity, frequency, or duration of the behavior decreases. Additionally, you will find the

Corrective Teaching Review

Devon enters your classroom one afternoon, and you greet him. He ignores you and says nothing as he rushes past. As the rest of the class visits quietly before the bell rings, you approach Devon at his desk to talk with him about his "greeting."

[OFFER INITIAL PRAISE OR EMPATHY]

"Devon, I'm glad you made it to class on time, and I appreciate you looking up just now."

[DESCRIBE THE INAPPROPRIATE BEHAVIOR]

"When I greeted you a moment ago, you rushed past me and didn't say anything."

[DESCRIBE THE APPROPRIATE BEHAVIOR]

"Whenever someone greets you, whether it's a teacher or other kids at school, it would be better if you would look at the person, smile, use a pleasant voice, and say something like 'Hello.'"

[GIVE A RATIONALE]

"Devon, when you greet people like that, they're more likely to see you as friendly and want to get to know you better."

[PRACTICE]

"Let's try that greeting again. This time, please greet me by using all the steps. We'll just pretend we're standing at the door like before. (Devon successfully practices the skill.)

Good job. Devon."

[USE A NEGATIVE CONSEQUENCE] *optional*

"Initially, Devon, you had some trouble greeting me, and we had to take some extra time and talk about a better way to greet others. Because of that, you missed out on some visiting time with your friends. But you did a nice job practicing the skill with me. And, you still have some time left to go talk with your friends. Devon, you did a really nice job listening to me. After the bell rings, let's start working on your vocabulary review."

most success when correcting behavior if you go into an interaction thinking it should always be a "conversation," not a "confrontation." Supports within the Well-Managed Schools program provide many options teachers can choose from to manage behavioral learning and increase student success. The graphic below represents how correction strategies can be used as a multi-tiered system of support.

Universal Interventions

- Be consistent and correct inappropriate behaviors when they are minor.

- Using preventive prompts, corrective strategies, guided self-correction, and de-escalation as needed often provides adequate support for the majority of students.

Secondary Interventions

- Guided self-correction and the use of frequent Corrective Teaching to address skill deficits provides additional supports to students who need more intensive interventions.

- Emphasize skill development.

- Use de-escalation as needed.

Tertiary Interventions

- A focus on specific and individualized target skills is often needed to meet the needs of students who require tertiary interventions.

- Use frequent Corrective Teaching for targeted skills.

- Use Corrective Teaching combined with negative consequences or within a motivation system.

- Monitoring and managing your own behavior is an important strategy to use at this tier. Managing your own emotions can become more difficult when working students at this level.

- Partner with outside supports (counselor, therapist, parents, special education staff, etc.).

- Use de-escalation as needed.

Final Thoughts

Up to now, we've stressed prevention – preventively teaching social skills, creating rules and procedures, setting clear behavioral expectations, catching kids being good, and addressing behaviors when they're small. When students ignore some or all of these strategies, you're likely to end up dealing with behaviors and situations that are more emotionally charged, more time consuming and disruptive, and more challenging to correct and change. By focusing on prevention and consistently correcting less serious inappropriate behavior, you ideally won't find yourself repeatedly referencing our next chapter – De-escalation.

De-escalation

Kendra and Molly are high school rivals who bad-mouth each other often. On one particular Monday, the girls traded insults and accusations throughout the morning because of a perceived slight at a weekend party. By the time both teens headed to Ms. Dawes' afternoon English class, their animosity was at a boiling point. Molly entered the classroom and put her books on her desk. As Kendra passed by, she knocked Molly's books to the floor and sarcastically said, "Oops. Sorrrryyyy!" The act startled Molly, who began crying as she scrambled to collect her things. Kendra stood and laughed. Seeing what happened, Ms. Dawes immediately approached both girls. Kneeling down next to Molly, she asked if she was okay, and then helped her pick up the books. Ms. Dawes told Molly to take her seat and that she would check on her in a few minutes. She then turned to Kendra and told her to sit at the table in the back of the room. After the bell rang and the rest of the students were in their seats, Ms. Dawes announced they were having Independent Time (an example of a preventive prompt; see Chapter 7) and told her class to get out their reading material. She then went to Kendra and began Corrective Teaching:

Ms. Dawes: "Kendra, I realize you're upset with Molly. But knocking her books to the floor and laughing at her is absolutely unacceptable."

Kendra: (Sighs loudly and turns away) "She asked for it."

Ms. Dawes: "Kendra, please look at me when I'm talking to you. It's important for you to listen and not interrupt me. Okay?"

Kendra looks back at Ms. Dawes.

Ms. Dawes: "Thank you for giving me your attention, Kendra. If you're having problems getting along with someone, you should talk to me or another adult who can help you resolve the situation and deal with your frustration. You…."

Kendra: (Interrupts Ms. Dawes and shouts) "That's crap. I can fight my own battles. Why are you always raggin' on me? Molly's been telling lies about me all day! Why aren't you talking to her?"

Ms. Dawes: "I will talk to Molly. But right now I'm talking to you. Please lower your voice and listen. I'm going to give you a couple of minutes to sit and think about making better choices. When I come back, we'll talk about being respectful to others. Okay?"

Kendra stomps her foot, mumbles, then nods "Yes."

Ms. Dawes checks to see that Molly has stopped crying and makes sure the other students are still on task. She then walks back to Kendra.

Ms. Dawes: "Thank you for sitting quietly and following my instructions. When you're willing to obey a request, it shows me you're listening and that's a sign of respect. That's good, Kendra. But you did knock Molly's books to the floor and disrupted the class. For that, you're going to serve a detention with me after school."

Kendra: (Leaps out of her chair and screams) "That's not fair! She (pointing at Molly) made me do it. She called me a slut and said I was a two-faced liar. What are you going to do about that? Molly gets away with everything. I'm the victim! I have practice tonight! I can't do detention!"

Kendra starts walking back and forth and sobbing.

Ms. Dawes turns to the other students, all of whom are staring back at Kendra, and prompts them to keep their faces forward and their eyes on their reading material. Then she looks at Kendra.

Ms. Dawes: "Kendra, you're pacing. Please stand still."

Kendra stops pacing.

Ms. Dawes: "Thanks for standing still. I know you're upset, but this situation isn't going to get any better by screaming. Try lowering your voice, please. Sounds like you think you're being treated unfairly. We certainly can talk about that at another time. Right now we're talking about what just happened."

Kendra stays quiet.

Ms. Dawes: "Kendra, it looks like you're making good choices. You're staying quiet and looking at me. This is going to get you back on task more quickly.

"Remember that whenever you earn a consequence, you should just look at the person, say 'Okay,' and not argue. Just like you're doing right now."

Kendra nods affirmatively.

Ms. Dawes: "Kendra, you've done a nice job of regaining your composure. I can see you've gotten your emotions under control, so you're not going to earn an office referral. But you still earned a detention for tonight for knocking Molly's books to the floor. Let's get back to class now and start the lesson."

Ms. Dawes also considers asking Molly and Kendra to stay after class so Kendra can apologize.

The Teachable Moment

The yelling. The crying. The fighting. The hating. Emotional meltdowns and blowups from students are often unpredictable and always unsettling. For these reasons, it's not surprising that some teachers fly by the seat of their pants or rely on gut instinct to try to calm or control emotionally distraught and/or physically violent students. Unfortunately, these teachers can get caught up in the emotion of the situation and lash out at students. While these responses may be understandable and seem natural given the tense nature of such situations, taking a course of action based on how one feels in the moment often only fuels the chaos. When teachers allow their emotions to dictate their actions, they find themselves in the Conflict Cycle (Chapter 13). Rather than shaping and directing a student's behavior in a positive direction, the opposite occurs. Teachers who are fortunate enough to sidestep that pitfall, but who "make it up as they go" because they lack any thoughtful strategy or method to reduce the tension, also prolong the misery. These teachers tend to get caught up in irrelevant details and discussions about blame, fairness, victimization, personality, or some other peripheral "fact" the student throws at them. These distractions, or excuses, take the focus off the only issue that matters: the student's out-of-control behavior.

In our opening example, the teacher was able to de-escalate Kendra's emotionally intense behaviors while still managing to keep everyone else on task because:

- The teacher saw the inappropriate behavior as an opportunity to teach a replacement skill.

- The teacher did not match or escalate her behaviors in response to the student's.

- The teacher, despite the student's attempts to deflect blame or justify her actions, taught to the behavior (both the appropriate and inappropriate), not the excuses or other extraneous issues.

- The teacher used corrective strategies, such as coupling statements and cool-down time, to calm the student first rather than trying to "teach over" the intensifying, interfering behaviors.

- The teacher had a procedure (Independent Time) to keep the rest of the class in line and on task.

In your classroom, there will be times when students become so agitated, defensive, or disruptive that you have to adjust your teaching. Generally, students start losing self-control when you're correcting a problem behavior or they're earning a negative consequence. These emotionally intense responses – arguing, shouting, crying, physically acting out, etc. – literally block a student from learning, so it becomes necessary to momentarily stop the Corrective Teaching or whatever type of correction you're doing with the student. You can't "teach over" these interfering behaviors. Students must be attentive and responsive. When they do not want to accept your instruction or feedback, they will let you know in ways that can be subtle and/or overt.

Some of what you might see and hear include:

> **Facial expressions** – looking away, glaring, rolling the eyes, frowning, and grinning

> **Verbal behaviors** – interrupting, arguing, swearing, talking to others, and mumbling

> **Body movements** – slouching, folding arms, turning and/or walking away, moving excessively, making noise with hands or other objects, gesturing with fingers or hands, and resting one's head on a desk or hand

> **Other behaviors** – not answering when asked to respond, sighing, crying, and laughing

These inappropriate responses or actions from students are the opposite of what they need to do to be successful: make eye contact, respond to questions or instructions, sit or stand quietly, and maintain a neutral facial expression. In this chapter, we'll look at strategies you can use to help students regain self-control and refocus their attention on your teaching efforts. These strategies give you options for calming students that are more positive and effective than simply making threats or issuing an office referral, choice that are too often overused and not necessarily the most constructive.

Prevent Emotional, Intense Behaviors

Ideally, the best way to handle outbursts and other emotionally intense episodes is to keep them from happening in the first place (although there can be circumstances in which such outbursts are unavoidable). Preventing frequent and severe misbehaviors requires the consistent use of the teaching strategies outlined in this book. These strategies help develop and strengthen relationships with students, making it more likely they will accept your instructions, corrections, or criticisms. Let's briefly review some of these preventive strategies:

Planned Teaching: Students are much more likely to meet your expectations and accept your feedback if you explain what it is you want from them. One way this can be accomplished is by preventively teaching them how to accept criticism or consequences. (We've paired both into one social skill, and its behavioral steps are outlined in Chapter 9.) All students are going to receive considerable feedback each day to help them develop a better, larger repertoire of skills and behaviors. By helping students learn how to accept criticism, you set them up for future success.

"Accepting Criticism or a Consequence" is a skill that many students may struggle with. For these students, frequent prompting (reminding them of behavioral expectations) before giving your feedback can help them internalize the skill. Also, it's important to remember that any time you're teaching or practicing social skills with students, you have to adjust your expectations based on each individual student's developmental level. Your expectations need to be realistic and reflect the student's abilities and familiarity with a particular skill.

As students begin to consistently use the skill of "Accepting Criticism or a Consequence," you should transition from simply requiring compliance to teaching self-management strategies. Teaching a range of skills (disagreeing or interrupting appropriately, controlling anger, giving negative feedback, expressing feelings appropriately, resolving conflicts, and using self-monitoring and self-reflection) will help students "read" social situations, review their options, and choose the best response (Tierney, Green, & Dowd, 2016).

Praise: In Chapter 12, we examined the various types of praise and how they can help maintain or increase appropriate behaviors. Praise is also an effective means to develop a relationship with your students. It can be your most powerful tool in changing behavior. Students who are frequently reinforced for positive behavior are less likely to act out to get your attention. If a student has a large "reinforcement reserve" (positive behaviors that were recognized with tangible rewards or activities, praise statements, privileges, or social reinforcers from others or the student), he or she is less likely to react inappropriately to a consequence or criticism. In order for students to develop their reinforcement reserve, you have to recognize and value their positive behaviors. Keep in mind, however, that if your praise sounds disingenuous, it won't be motivating to students. Likewise, if you make only general statements about their positive behaviors but never use specific or Effective Praise, students may not know what you're reinforcing and they won't know what behaviors to repeat.

Behavior Correction: These approaches (outlined in the previous chapter – modeling, corrective prompts, corrective strategies, guided self-correction, and Corrective Teaching) should be utilized whenever minor misbehaviors occur. Intervening early, when behaviors are "small," will help students learn your expectations and tolerances, and possibly prevent an escalation of inappropriate behavior.

In order for behavior correction approaches to have the desired effect of reducing the frequency, severity, and duration of emotional outbursts, they have to be used frequently, not sporadically. If students respond to your criticisms by asking, "Why are you talking to me about this today?" or respond to your praise by saying, "You've never thanked me before," that's an indication you're probably not being proactive or using corrective approaches often enough. For example, one day you finally decide you've had it with a student's disruptive behavior, so you address the situation using guided self-correction. But you have never used that strategy with any student and never bothered to correct that particular misbehavior before (in essence, you've changed your tolerance level without communicating it to the students). As a result, more confusion and frustration is created. It's likely the student will escalate the behavior because he doesn't understand why you are calling him out. Your actions may be seen as arbitrary and unfair. And because the student doesn't understand what his behavioral mistake was, it will be more difficult to problem-solve the situation, which is the whole point of using guided self-correction. This lack of consistency and preparation creates a reactive environment when your goal is to have a proactive one.

While it is important to use all of the behavior correction approaches consistently and frequently, it's just as critical to evaluate whether or not those strategies are producing the desired outcome. If one strategy doesn't seem to work with a particular student, but you continually use it, nothing will change. If you are not teaching students the right skills in the right way in response to the problem, they won't be able to overcome their behavioral mistakes.

You have to be willing to adjust your strategy when correcting behavioral mistakes, especially if the behaviors intensify or become repetitive. Sometimes the real problem lies with the antecedents or consequences of the behavior. Maybe something in the environment is working against you – a rule, procedure, expectation, etc. – or the consequence you are using has no relevance or is not motivating to the student. When it comes to evaluating outcomes and measuring the effectiveness of your intervention efforts, you have to look at the entire context, not just certain elements or events in isolation. We'll take a closer look at how to evaluate the effectiveness of your intervention efforts in Chapter 16.

Help Students Regain Self-Control

As we noted, the total elimination of intense and inappropriate behaviors is next to impossible. Some students are going to lose it, and when they do, you can't ignore the behavior or automatically push the students off on someone else. Your first objective has to be helping the student regain self-control, if you can, before attempting to correct whatever behavioral mistake was made. In the previous chapter, we introduced several corrective strategies to help you de-escalate tensions: cool-down time, coupling statements, reality statements/reasons, empathy, and specific praise. Let's look at how these strategies were used in the classroom by reviewing how Ms. Dawes dealt with Kendra's escalating behaviors:

> **Cool-down time** – Kendra was visibly upset and interrupted the Corrective Teaching interaction, so Ms. Dawes gave her "a couple minutes to think about making better choices." This was enough time for Ms. Dawes to collect her thoughts and redirect the other students, while giving Kendra some much-needed cooling-off time.

> **Coupling statements** – When Kendra "lost it" (sobbing and pacing) after earning detention as a negative consequence, Ms. Dawes addressed the most disruptive behavior first – the pacing – by using a coupling statement: "Kendra, you're pacing. Please stand still." This explicit instruction told Kendra

exactly what behavior needed to stop and what replacement behavior she needed to use. For Ms. Dawes to continue Corrective Teaching, she first needed Kendra to stop or diminish the behavior that was causing the most interference.

Reality statements/reasons – Kendra felt disrespected by Molly and then by her teacher. Kendra needed to understand that respect is a two-way street and that in order to be respected by others, she had to be respectful of them. Ms. Dawes used this rationale with Kendra: "When you're willing to obey a request, it shows me you are listening, and that's a sign of respect."

Empathy – Ms. Dawes acknowledged Kendra's frustration before starting the Corrective Teaching interaction when she said, "Kendra, I realize you're upset with Molly." She empathized with Kendra later in the interaction when she said, "Kendra, I know you think you're being treated unfairly."

Specific praise – Several times, Ms. Dawes pointed out the positive steps Kendra was taking even though some of her behaviors were still intense and inappropriate. Examples of these specific praise statements included: "Thank you for sitting quietly and following my instructions," and "You're doing a great job listening. You're not interrupting me or looking away."

All of these corrective strategies help shape behavior and encourage self-control. As always, it's important to be aware of your own behaviors throughout the interaction – use a calm voice tone, avoid harsh, demanding instructions, and pause often to allow the student to respond. There may be times when you will need to talk while the student is talking, but be careful not to "talk over" him or her. If the student raises his or her voice, lower yours; by modeling an appropriate conversational tone, you may influence the student to lower his or her voice, or the student may have to quiet down just so he or she can hear you. When a student is emotionally intense and argumentative, demands and accusations will be hurled. Avoid responding directly to this "content"; otherwise, you'll find yourself in a power struggle with the student. A better strategy is to deal with the inappropriate arguing using the techniques that were just described. Even if a student has a valid issue to discuss, addressing it at that moment might reinforce the negative behaviors the student used to bring up his or her concerns.

Here is an example of avoiding content while targeting the misbehavior:

Kadeem yells, "You're so unfair! How come you like everyone else better than me?"

You respond by saying, "I can see you have some issues you'd like to discuss with me and I'd be happy to set a time later today for us to talk **(Empathy)**. But instead of trying to talk about it now, please be quiet and listen **(Coupling Statement)** so we can finish this and move on with the class **(Rationale)**."

This shaping process should continue as long as the student demonstrates improvement in his or her behavior. The more praise you can provide the student to further motivate behavior change, the better. You shouldn't withhold praise because a student doesn't do every step of a skill exactly right or to your liking. Whatever progress is made in a positive direction, even if a student does only some of the steps to a skill or behavior or reduces his emotional intensity even a little, acknowledge the effort.

Sometimes, emotionally intense behaviors will continue or escalate and progress can't be made, or a student will simply substitute one inappropriate behavior for another. Then an office referral may be the next step. If other students' safety becomes a concern or their academic needs are jeopardized because so much of your time and attention is being directed elsewhere, the office referral is an appropriate course of action to take. That being said, your goal still should be to keep the student in the classroom, if at all possible, so he or she doesn't lose even more valuable instruction time.

Complete Corrective Teaching

Remember, students often lose self-control and demonstrate emotionally intense behaviors during the Corrective Teaching process. These outbursts can be so disorienting that it's easy to forget why you were correcting a student in the first place. When you manage to help a student regain his or her composure using the various corrective approaches and strategies described, it's important that you wrap up the interaction by teaching an appropriate skill, whether it's "Accepting Criticism or a Consequence," "Following Instructions," or "Staying on Task." Sometimes teachers are so relieved a student regained self-control or are fearful the student will "go off" again, they let the whole issue drop without any proper resolution. That's a mistake because it's as if the student is "rewarded" (because no consequence is given) for the emotional outburst. Finishing Corrective Teaching is essential, and there are three basic ways to do that after the student regains self-control. Your options are:

Option 1: Teach in response to the escalated behavior and the behavior that led to the original correction.

Option 2: Teach in response only to the escalated behavior.

Option 3: Return to the original correction.

Whatever choice you make, you must complete the Corrective Teaching steps, including giving a consequence for the behavior you choose to address. The following pages illustrate each option and how they look and sound.

Option 1: Teach in response to the escalated behavior and the behavior that led to the original correction.

Choosing this option means you will complete two Corrective Teaching interactions. Your decision to focus on the escalated behavior as well as the original behavioral mistake should be based on the student's need to learn skills for both and his or her ability to process this amount of information. One interaction will focus on the original skill deficit. In Kendra's case, this was her aggressive behavior in knocking Molly's books to the floor. To determine the other skill to teach, consider these factors:

- **The antecedents to the behavior.** For example, if the escalated behavior occurred during the "consequence" step, you may want to teach the student how to accept a consequence or how to disagree appropriately. If the student went ballistic when you asked him or her to practice a skill, you might want to teach how to follow instructions. Teaching the student how to accept criticism is logical if the student engaged in emotionally intense behaviors during Step 2, when you were describing the inappropriate behavior.

- **The student's individual needs.** Ask yourself, "What skill does this student frequently have trouble with?"; "What skill will provide the greatest help in different situations?"; and "What can I teach that will allow this student to better manage his or her behavior?" These questions will help you choose an appropriate skill that still addresses the problem or issue, especially with students who have progressed beyond compliance-based skills but need to develop more self-management skills.

- **The student's need to improve on basic skills.** Typically, the second Corrective Teaching interaction involves accepting criticism or a consequence. Most escalated behavior comes from students who are still in the acquisition stage of social skills learning. In order for these students to progress to higher-level skills, they need to increase their fluency or ability to use the critical skills of "Accepting Criticism or a Consequence," and "Following Instructions."

Once you decide to teach a student two skills and know which skills they are, go back to the steps of Corrective Teaching. You'll start by using corrective strategies (cool-down time, coupling statements, reality statements/reasons, empathy, and specific praise) to help the student regain self-control. You'll teach in response to the escalated behaviors first before addressing the original misbehavior.

Here is an example:

"Before we can talk about staying on task, Elizabeth, we first need to discuss how you just accepted that criticism. **(Transition Statement)** When I tried to talk to you about being off task, you argued with me. **(Description of Inappropriate Behavior)**

"Remember, whenever someone gives you criticism, you need to look at them, say 'Okay,' and not argue. **(Description of Appropriate Behavior)**

"When you can accept criticism without arguing, you won't make the situation worse." **(Rationale)**

After successfully dealing with the escalated behaviors, turn your attention to the issue of staying on task (the original reason you started Corrective Teaching). Include a preventive prompt to increase the student's chances for success in accepting the rest of your criticism and consequence.

"Elizabeth, you'll get another chance to practice how to accept criticism because we need to finish talking about you being off task. Remember to look at me and not argue, okay?" **(Prompt)**

Complete the original Corrective Teaching sequentially:

"Let's talk about staying on task. Remember to think about the steps you have to follow to complete the task, stay focused, and work until you're instructed to stop. **(Description of Appropriate Behavior)**

"That way, you will probably finish your essay and not have to take it home with you. **(Rationale)**

"Let's practice staying on task. I'm going to go check Tyrell's work. While I'm gone, start working and remain focused on finishing your essay." **(Practice)**

Elizabeth stays on task and completes her work.

"Elizabeth, great job staying on task! You worked quietly on your essay and finished another paragraph. Way to go!

"Because you initially had some problems staying on task and accepting criticism, you weren't able to finish your essay in class. You'll have to take it home and finish it for homework. But since you practiced both those skills so well, your essay won't be counted as late. **(Consequence)**

"Thanks for working so well with me. Since there are a couple of minutes left in class, why don't you see if you can get another paragraph done before the bell rings."

Option 2: Teach in response only to the escalated behavior.

Sometimes you may decide that the escalated behavior represents a greater skill deficit and requires more attention than the original inappropriate behavior. Therefore, you're going to focus only on the escalated behaviors. In some instances, your past experience with the student, as well as the facts of the current situation, will tell you that the original behavioral mistake is just an antecedent to the "real" problem – accepting your feedback about any type of mistake. You can address the original issue at another time through a delayed practice or by using Effective Praise when the student demonstrates the skill appropriately. In Elizabeth's example, you might notice her staying on task at another time and reinforce her use of the skill then.

Here is an example of using Corrective Teaching when you focus only on the escalated behavior:

"Elizabeth, instead of talking about staying on task, it looks like we need to discuss how you accepted that criticism. **(Transition Statement)**

"Just now, when I tried to talk to you about being off task, you argued with me. **(Description of Inappropriate Behavior)**

"Remember that whenever you get criticism, you should just look at the person, say 'Okay,' and not argue. Just like you're doing right now. **(Description of Appropriate Behavior)**

"Nice job, Elizabeth. You accepted my criticism without arguing! When you can do that you have a lot more time to spend on your work. Does that make sense?" **(Rationale)**

Elizabeth acknowledges by nodding "Yes."

"Super. Since you had difficulty accepting criticism the first time about being off task, we had to spend some time talking about the skill. So, you lost quite a bit of work time and you'll probably have to finish your assignment at home. But Elizabeth, since you did such a nice job of listening and paying attention, I won't count that assignment as late. **(Consequence)**

"Now why don't you get back to your essay. You might still be able to finish it before the end of class. If you need my help on anything, just raise your hand."

Option 3: Return to the original correction.

This third choice works best if the escalated behavior was fairly brief and not too intense. If you can help the student regain self-control with a few prompts, cues, and/or coupling statements, then simply turn your attention to completing the original Corrective Teaching interaction. It's a good idea to "pick up where you left off," unless that involves describing what the student did inappropriately. If you "rehash" the behavioral mistake, you may risk inciting additional unwanted behaviors. When escalated behaviors occur during the "consequences" step, include a preventive prompt before you return to the original teaching interaction. This prepares the student to accept the consequences appropriately. Here is an example of how a Corrective Teaching interaction might start:

"Elizabeth, just a moment ago you were looking around the room, tapping your pencil, and yawning." **(Description of Inappropriate Behavior)**

Elizabeth starts arguing.

"Elizabeth, you're talking; please be quiet. **(Coupling Statement/ Pause)** Great. You're quiet. **(Praise)**

"Can you keep looking at me too, please? **(Prompt)** Thanks, Elizabeth, for looking at me. **(Praise)** I know this may be difficult, but the sooner we finish discussing it, the sooner you can finish the assignment and be done with it. **(Empathy/Rationale)**

"Instead of looking down at your feet, look up at me. That way I know you're listening. **(Coupling Statement/Rationale)** Nice job of making eye contact and following that instruction. Let's go on, okay? Remember to just look at me and say 'Okay.'" **(Praise/ Preventive Prompt)**

After Elizabeth regains self-control, go back to the reason why you started Corrective Teaching:

"Nice job, Elizabeth. Whenever you're given a task, get all the materials you need, work quietly, focus on the task until it's complete, and then let me know when you're finished. **(Description of Appropriate Behavior)**

"If you can do that, you'll probably finish the work a lot quicker and move on to something you enjoy, like reading your novel. Does that make sense? Tell me how you're going to stay on task." **(Rationale)**

Elizabeth acknowledges that she understands the rationale and then lists the steps to staying on task.

"Okay, let's practice. I'm going to go help Tyrell. While I'm over there, you'll need to practice staying on task by finishing the paragraph you're working on right now. Okay? I'll be back shortly to see how you did." **(Practice)**

Elizabeth works quietly on her writing assignment.

"Great job staying on task! You stayed on task and got that paragraph written!

"Since you had trouble staying on task, and we had to discuss and practice it, you didn't have as much time to read your novel. But because you did practice staying on task so nicely, you don't have as much of your assignment left to do. **(Consequence)**

"Awesome effort, Elizabeth! Now let's get ready to go to lunch."

Using de-escalation to manage emotionally intense situations provides students with a process for recovering self-control before you have to resort to an office referral. The number and type of strategies you use to try to maintain appropriate behavior and keep the student in class should be based on the intensity, frequency, and duration of the student's behavior. However, there is no magic number of strategies or sequences that will change behavior faster. Decisions on which strategies to use are based on how the student behaves, how the teacher responds, and prior experience. The teaching process should begin only after the student shows compliance by accepting responsibility for his or her behavior, practicing a replacement behavior, and showing quality components that include using a calm voice, making eye contact, and demonstrating appropriate posture. The following figure represents the de-escalation process for managing behavioral learning.

De-Escalation

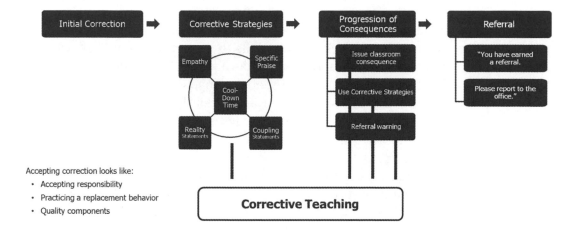

Accepting correction looks like:
- Accepting responsibility
- Practicing a replacement behavior
- Quality components

Additional Considerations

The skill(s) you teach to students should be the one(s) that will be most beneficial to helping them overcome their behavioral mistakes, so structure your teaching according to the individual situation. That may mean rearranging some of the steps to make your teaching more effective. Also remember that the size of the consequence you use should be in proportion to the frequency and severity of the behavior. (Refer to Chapter 8, "Understanding and Giving Consequences," for guidance.)

Each student has different needs, so view each student individually and teach according to his or her needs and the behavioral outcome you are trying to achieve. Don't be too rule-governed or try to follow an exact procedure with every student and situation. Behavior is not an isolated or static event; exchanges occur in a dynamic context, with each aspect related to those that precede and follow it. By recognizing behavior as an interactional, developmental process, you can modify and customize your teaching to meet the needs of all students.

Students also may need additional teaching on how to cope with anger or emotions, especially at the secondary and tertiary levels of intervention. Self-control or coping strategies are a great way to reduce the frequency and intensity of student outbursts and should be taught to students proactively. Many students who have emotional outbursts lack the key skills to control their own behaviors and successfully resolve conflict during times of emotional distress. Self-control strategies are essential components for these students because they enable students who previously were incapable of getting their needs met in emotionally intense situations to begin to cope with stress and successfully change their behaviors and resolve conflict. By using self-control strategies, students are able to reduce the frequency, severity, and duration of emotional outbursts that occur when they encounter seemingly insurmountable dilemmas. Students will inevitably continue to struggle in these situations if they don't have the necessary skills for controlling their emotions.

When teachers and school staff are successful in teaching self-control strategies, students will progress beyond the need to rely on adult authority for behavior control. If students can implement self-control strategies properly, they will have learned to manage their own behavior, control their impulses and feelings, live by rules and values, make constructive rather than destructive decisions, and deal with others in their lives in a more positive manner. Ultimately, one of the most crucial goals for every student in school is learning to correctly choose and use a self-control strategy, without cues or prompts, as they begin to identify and anticipate circumstances that could lead to emotional upheaval. Some common strategies you can teach to students are:

Deep Breathing
- Slowly inhale through your nose.
- Hold your breath for three seconds.
- Exhale through your mouth.
- Repeat until you feel yourself calming down.
- Inhale good thoughts; exhale angry thoughts.

Counting
- Count slowly from one to ten (or count by 5's to 100, count backwards from 100, count by 20's, etc.).

- Continue your counting, but reverse it.
- Repeat until you feel yourself calming down.

Saying the ABC's

- Say the ABC's forward or backward, sing the alphabet song, or use the ABC game (a is for apple, b is for banana, c is for carrot).
- Make sure you do this slowly.
- Speak quietly so no one can hear.
- Repeat until you feel yourself calming down.

Thought Stopping

- Stop whatever you are doing.
- Imagine a STOP sign in front of your face.
- Picture all eight sides of the stop sign.
- Visualize the letters S-T-O-P.
- Clear your mind of all thoughts.
- Begin thinking again only when you have positive thoughts.

Muscle Relaxation

- Tense the muscles in your feet first; hold for five seconds and release.
- Breathe in and out slowly.
- Tense your leg and foot muscles, hold for five seconds, and release.
- Continue to tense your muscles, moving upward from your feet and legs until all the muscles in your body have been tensed for five seconds and released.

Visual Imagery

- Close your eyes.
- Imagine a happy/calming place.
- Visualize what you are seeing.
- Think about what you are smelling, who is with you, and what you hear.
- Do not open your eyes until you feel calm.

Positive Self-Talk

- Identify positive statements you've said to yourself prior to a situation where you might become angry.
- Repeat one of these positive statements when you are becoming upset.
- Use a statement you believe in.
- Repeat the statement to yourself at least five times.
- Identify positive ways to handle the situation.

Isometrics

- Sit down.
- Press your hands firmly together.
- Hold for a count of 10.
- Release to a count of five.
- Repeat as necessary.

Anger Diary/Journaling

- Request permission to write in your journal.
- Record your thoughts, feelings, behaviors, and specific ways you plan to handle the situation.
- Continue until you are calm.
- Share what you wrote with a trusted adult.

Ideally, self-control or coping strategies are things students can do at their desks without requiring a specific item, person, or place. However, there may be instances in secondary or tertiary interventions when you have a student go to a specific place or use an item to calm down. Over time, it is best to shape these strategies so students can better generalize them to future situations and those that occur outside the school environment.

Referrals

This chapter emphasized how to prevent or de-escalate behaviors that interfere with the learning process. When these strategies are effective, students regain self-control so you can complete your teaching and they can remain in your class. However, there will be situations when students won't respond to your efforts. When this happens, they need to leave the classroom to receive additional, individualized attention from an administrator.

It's your decision when to start the referral process. We've already discussed how the safety of other students may be the tipping point in issuing a referral. Another cue that may tell you it's time to move on is the behavior of other students. If they're getting active or restless and you've prompted them to MYOB (Mind Your Own Behavior), but five minutes later they're all chatting or trying to involve themselves in the situation, it means you've given too much time and attention to one individual. You have to find a way to wrap it up or come to a resolution, and that might involve an office referral. Another factor to consider is the frequency, severity, and duration of the behavior and whether or not the student shows any progress toward the goal of regaining self-control.

The most logical time to issue a referral is when a student displays behavior that continues or escalates during Corrective Teaching. If you perceive the behavior as dangerous to the student, you, or others, all the Corrective Teaching steps should be bypassed and the student should immediately be referred to the office. Examples of behavior that would result in an immediate referral include, but are not limited to, verbal or physical abuse or assault, major destruction of property, and being under the influence of drugs or alcohol. Most likely, your school or school district already has a list of major offenses that automatically require the removal of a student from a classroom.

When you feel your efforts to motivate behavioral change are futile, or the behavior continues to escalate, you need to refer the student to the office. Here is one example of how a structured referral process might look and sound:

David is a student who forgot his homework. The teacher approaches him as he stands by his desk to discuss the situation and David starts arguing and pointing his finger.

> **Teacher:** "David, you're talking loudly. A better choice would be to be quiet and listen."

> **David:** Reacts by lowering his voice, crossing his arms, turning his back on the teacher, and continuing to argue.

Teacher: "Thank you for lowering your voice. You're continuing to talk. Please be quiet and listen." (Pause)

David: Ignores the teacher's instructions and continues his disruptive behaviors.

Teacher: "It's great that you're standing still and staying right here, but you're still arguing. We could take care of this a lot quicker if you would be quiet and listen." (Pause)

David: Continues to ignore the instruction and argue loudly.

Teacher: "Because this is taking a lot of time and you're not listening, you've earned a detention with me during lunch."

NOTE: In this situation, the teacher first tries using a moderate consequence in an effort to motivate the student to stop the inappropriate behaviors. A moderate consequence can involve the loss of a privilege (recess time, computer time, staying after school, or a note or call home to parents), or anything that reflects the seriousness of the student's behavior.

When the behaviors do not change, let the student know an office referral is possible. This indicates the seriousness of the situation and what will happen if the behavior doesn't stop. By telling the student what consequence he or she will earn for not regaining self-control, you help establish a link between the behavior and the consequence. The student should realize he or she determines what happens next – either stop the negative behavior or earn the negative consequence. By understanding this basic concept – that the student can control the outcome of a situation by controlling his or her behavior – the student hopefully will choose to avoid the major consequence of an office referral.

David: Continues his escalated behaviors.

Teacher: "If you continue to argue with me and not follow my instructions, you will need to report to the office." (Pause)

NOTE: The student should be referred to the office if he or she continues to behave inappropriately after you have described the potential negative consequence. At this point, your attempts to help the student regain self-control have been unsuccessful, so in fairness to the student and the other students, a referral is necessary. When giving the actual office referral, tell the student he or she earned a major consequence and to report to the office. Ask the student if he or she needs help getting to the office. The student no longer has the option of staying in the classroom, but might not get up and leave on his or her own. In such instances, rely on the predetermined procedures that are in place for such situations, which may include calling the school resource officer or an administrator to your room.

David: Remains standing and argues.

Teacher: "David, for arguing and not following instructions, you need to report to the office. Can you get there by yourself or do you need some help?"

David: "Fine!" (Leaves the room, slamming the door on his way out.)

Teacher: (Calls the office via the intercom) "David Altman has been referred to the office. He's on his way."

OR

David: Sits down in his chair, crosses his arms, looks away, and says nothing.

Teacher: (Calls the office via the intercom) "David Altman has been referred to the office. He needs assistance."

Giving the student the choice to report to the office on his or her own, or with assistance, gives that young person one last opportunity to save face, make a good decision, and demonstrate a willingness to finally turn the behavior around. Oftentimes, you will be so frustrated, you could care less about giving the student a choice. But remember, you want to create an environment where making good decisions is valued, so take advantage of any opportunity to empower students to do just that.

Hopefully, a student will quietly leave the classroom and report directly to the office. Should he or she refuse, your main concern has to be the well-being of others. It's unproductive (at best) to try to teach the student additional skills at this time. If you pay attention to his or her refusal to leave, you only reinforce that behavior and give the student an audience in front of the other students. As long as he or she is not disturbing others, the student should remain in your class until an administrator arrives. (Of course, this is assuming that an administrator or crisis interventionist is in the building and will arrive within minutes of the referral.)

In the event that a student not only refuses to leave the classroom, but also becomes increasingly violent or destructive, your best option is to get everyone else out. Moving students to a hallway, media center, or multipurpose room is preferable to attempting physical restraint or allowing the out-of-control student to show off his or her outrageous behavior in front of peers. Leaving the student alone may help de-escalate the behavior, and you will ensure no one is at risk of getting hurt.

Repeated Referrals

Despite all your efforts to be proactive, teach skills, and use Corrective Teaching and other strategies, there will be some students who simply won't turn their behavior around.

To help these students find success, it's essential that everyone who has contact with them – teachers, administrators, counselors, coaches, etc. – re-examine the way they interact with these students and reconsider how to better meet their needs. The questions that should be asked include:

- Are we teaching the student the right skills?

- Are we providing enough reinforcement when the student makes good choices?

- Have we really stopped behaviors that were inappropriate and taught alternative behaviors?

- Are we using consequences that are meaningful to the student, or have the consequences become so severe the student feels hopeless?

- Does the student feel helpless because his or her life experience has been one of struggles and screw-ups?

- Are we using the appropriate level of support in our multitiered system?

When you work with students with repeated referrals, try to determine if they have a skill deficit or a performance deficit. A skill deficit means the student simply does not know how to perform the desired skill. Students with skill deficits have to be re-taught the skills and require more practice. A logical time to practice is when they are in the administrator's office. The key to helping these students overcome their behavioral mistakes is to constantly reinforce any steps they take in a positive direction. It's also better to deal with their small misbehaviors before they escalate to the point where they've gotten on your "very last nerve" and your response is more hostile than helpful.

Students who have a performance deficit understand how to use a skill; they just lack the motivation to use it consistently. These students tend to have a different outlook or perspective, so they don't view their behavior as a refusal to do something. For example, when a student raises his voice to you, you might consider that behavior to be an act of insubordination. You might also think that student doesn't want to talk to you in a respectful manner. The student, however, might feel that every adult just wants to tell him or her what to do, so the student decides to talk back.

Helping students who have performance deficits requires a comprehensive and more intensive intervention effort. Seeking advice or help from others who know and care about the student is often necessary and beneficial. If your school has a Student Assistance Team (SAT), get them involved. The SAT typically consists of a counselor, special education teacher/coordinator, administrator, school psychologist, and/or general education teacher. They can give you more insight into the student's needs and help you employ a more effective intervention strategy. And never forget the role of parents. If possible, they should be involved. For starters, they may provide answers or explanations as to why their child struggles with a particular behavior or skill. Another advantage of parental involvement is that they can offer reinforcement and encouragement at home, so the student receives consistent feedback and much-needed extra help.

Referrals

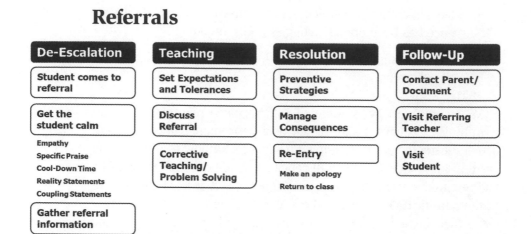

De-Escalation	Teaching	Resolution	Follow-Up
Student comes to referral	**Set Expectations and Tolerances**	**Preventive Strategies**	**Contact Parent/ Document**
Get the student calm	**Discuss Referral**	**Manage Consequences**	**Visit Referring Teacher**
Empathy Specific Praise Cool-Down Time Reality Statements Coupling Statements	**Corrective Teaching/ Problem Solving**	**Re-Entry** Make an apology Return to class	**Visit Student**
Gather referral information			

Whether the student has a skill deficit or a performance deficit, the application of strategies and support through the Well-Managed Schools program can provide the necessary motivation to promote behavioral change. Students with multiple referrals often represent less than 5 percent of your school's population, but require 80 percent of your time to effectively manage their behavior. By focusing on a system of supports that promotes teaching, you can better effect long-term change. This is better than trying to use an aversive quick-fix that results in little to no positive change. Additionally, the multi-tiered nature of the Well-Managed Schools program allows teachers to be the primary change agents for students and provides a roadmap of strategies for obtaining positive behavioral outcomes. Multi-tiered strategies are a starting point for student support. Many of these can be supplemented with check-in/check-out supports, motivation systems, or individualized plans. However, the focus should always be on providing students with the supports necessary to promote positive change. Then the supports can be faded as they become unnecessary.

Final Thoughts

You may find that your most powerful tool in preventing emotionally intense behavior is consistent teaching and recognition of a student's efforts. Clearly communicating your expectations and following up with praise and Corrective Teaching show your concern and fairness, and help build strong relationships with students. These relationships, in turn, may help students bring their behavior under control in stressful situations. At the very least, even if you are unsuccessful in helping a student remain in your class after he or she has lost self-control, the student's return to your room will be easier because your relationship with the student has remained intact.

Communicating
with Stakeholders

A T FIRST GLANCE, YOU MAY THINK A CHAPTER ON HOW to reach out to parents (Chapter 15) has no relevance to a chapter on evaluating classroom and school management efforts (Chapter 16) and vice versa. Yet in many ways, they are more connected than one might assume.

In an odd way, when you're dealing with issues of parental involvement and evaluation, you are confronted with the same challenge: staying power. Research shows that parental involvement with schools declines as children mature and move into junior high and high school. As an educator, how do you reach out to parents who are pulled in many directions and who, by choice or circumstance, view their connection to school as either unnecessary or less vital?

When assessing school management practices, we know the most useful and effective evaluations are continuous. They don't happen once a semester or once a year, and the results don't get shoved into a file. The data are continually gathered and used to formulate new strategies and improve existing ones. Yet, like parents, educators have many demands and responsibilities placed on them. Over time, the attention paid to specific intervention strategies can diminish. Motivations fade, new priorities take precedence, or a presumption of success or failure leads to infrequent and incorrect assessments. Sustaining parental involvement and sustaining evaluation efforts may be two of the most persistent and personal challenges you face.

Partnering with Parents and Guardians

Schools have a responsibility to reach out to families and build relationships with parents and guardians, preferably before academic or behavioral problems arise. Yet, attempts to be proactive are often neglected or are simply ineffective. When schools fail or wait to communicate with parents, for whatever reason, until after a problem develops, problem resolution tends to be awkward and time intensive. When both parties are virtual strangers, there is a lack of familiarity that can breed more suspicion than trust. In some cases, no amount of bridge-building will bring parents to the table.

Parental inclusion and involvement in school life is universally regarded as a win-win situation for the entire learning community. One benefit for schools is that parents represent a vast talent pool from which to draw volunteers, mentors, guest speakers, and classroom aides who can enliven and enrich the learning experience for all students. More tangible benefits can be seen in the classroom. Domina (2005), for example, found that children have fewer behavior problems when their parents volunteer in the school or at school-related activities, check homework, and engage in other parental-involvement activities. There are rewards for parents, too. They learn more about the school and often gain useful knowledge about valuable health and social services. The local community also benefits. As relationships strengthen, there's a greater sense of shared purpose, which can increase support for other economic and development initiatives (Wynn, Meyer, & Richards-Schuster, 2000).

According to McNeal (1999), involved parents can influence their children's behavior in three ways. Through words and deeds that communicate the importance of education, parents can socialize their children to understand the value of schoolwork. Involved parents also exert social control. This is done through the relationships parents forge with their children's teachers, classmates, and other parents. These relationships make it easier for parents to monitor their children's activities. Finally, involved parents benefit from inside information. Thanks to the relationships they've developed with stakeholders in the school, these parents learn and exchange important information. As a result, when an academic or behavioral problem arises, they are aware of it sooner and know what resources and solutions are available much more so than their uninvolved counterparts.

While few can argue against the concept of having parents engaged in school life, many educators struggle with exactly how to make it a reality. Those new to the profession find it to be especially difficult. In the 2004-2005 MetLife Survey of the American Teacher, more than 30 percent of new teachers (five years of experience or less) reported that their greatest challenge was communicating with and engaging parents. That sentiment was shared by 34 percent of principals. In addition, 20 percent of new teachers characterized their relationships with parents as very or somewhat unsatisfying.

Identifying Roadblocks to Parental Involvement

Oftentimes, adverse sociological and economic factors interfere with parent-teacher relationships. The home lives of students vary greatly in terms of stability and degrees of dysfunction, which, in turn, influence how willing or able parents are to communicate and get involved. And it's not just socioeconomic issues. For many parents, the barrier can be emotional. Contact with the school can be fraught with anxiety and even fear. If parents' experiences as students were less than ideal, they may come to school with preconceived negative expectations. The same is true for parents who may have had previous run-ins with school staff that left them bitter and disappointed. The perceived slights of the past, even those unrelated to you or your school, can strain current attempts to forge productive working relationships. And sometimes, it isn't past or personal problems or external pressures. The issue may simply be the age of the student; as children grow older, parental involvement declines (Catsambis & Garland, 1997; Crosnoe, 2001). Explanations as to why this happens vary. The MetLife Survey, for example, found that secondary schoolteachers don't ask parents to be involved as frequently as their elementary school colleagues. As for the parents of older youth, many tell us they feel overwhelmed by other responsibilities. In addition, many feel their child's success is now less a matter of their personal involvement and is more dependent on the abilities and responsibilities of their teen.

We understand that some of the obstacles you face may seem insurmountable, despite your best intentions and efforts. But rather than using the bleakness of a situation as an excuse to stop trying, you must realize that change is sometimes slow and circumstances can change. Just as you wouldn't give up on a child, you shouldn't forsake trying to reach out to parents. Here are a few characteristics of parents that make school-home partnerships especially difficult. We've included suggestions on how to respond to these special challenges so they do not become even more negative:

- **Apathetic** – When it appears that parents have given up on their children and make statements to that regard, it is important to say and do things that model hopefulness. Try to redirect their pessimism by asking questions or making comments that encourage positive responses. Seize on the slightest hint of enthusiasm or interest they show and reinforce it with positive statements of your own.

- **Unreliable** – The best approach with parents who seem less than dependable is to use preventive and educational methods. In other words, let them know what you need and when and why you need it. Before you put a label like "unreliable" on a parent, make an effort to see if there is an underlying reason that could explain the behavior. For example, a parent who relies on public transportation or works more than one job may have trouble attending school events in the evenings. In these situations, be open to alternative solutions, such as meeting at the family's home or "meeting" over the telephone or online. Remember, some parents who had negative school experiences may not feel welcome in the school or may feel intimidated. If they don't think they have anything to contribute, their motivation will be limited. As always, be welcoming and reinforcing. Offer suggestions or meaningful roles or tasks they feel comfortable with and capable of doing.

- **Hostile and Uncooperative** – The same strategies you use to calm an emotionally intense student can be applied to angry parents. Your first objective is to remain calm and professional. Try to avoid aggressive posturing or accusatory statements that only feed the Conflict Cycle. Rather, use empathy to redirect attention where it should be – on resolving a problem, not placing blame. If you feel a situation is becoming too explosive, end the meeting and have an administrator or colleague mediate subsequent meetings. Using a mediator is better than cutting off all contact. You want to continue to show parents that despite your differences, their input remains valuable. If you seem to have more than your share of angry parents, you may want to seek feedback from colleagues about your professional demeanor and image. Perhaps there is something you do that is alienating to others.

- **Emotionally Disturbed or Physically Distressed** – Behaviors that indicate mental health disorders or substance abuse problems raise all sorts of questions and issues that are beyond the scope of this chapter. For that reason, we recommend you avoid playing the role of counselor. Instead, refer parents to a school or community social worker who can tell them about public and private agencies that can provide relevant services. For their children's sake, it's vitally important that you give them the empathy and support they need.

- **Abusive and Neglectful** – If you discover that a parent or primary caregiver is abusing or neglecting a child, immediately contact the proper authorities and agencies. Follow your school's policies or procedures for handling such instances.

The obstacles and situations just described do not discriminate. They're found in schools serving urban, suburban, exurban, and rural populations. Fortunately, many of the barriers that keep parents and educators apart do not require the investment of time, energy, or outside assistance that others do. In fact, most hurdles to better school-family relationships can be overcome simply by making communication more open and frequent.

Paving a Way Toward Better Relationships

Schools tend to take a narrow approach to parent involvement by focusing on one kind of activity (homework hotlines or parent workshops), or emphasizing the needs of the school rather than the needs of parents or students (Burch & Palanki, 1994; Mannan & Blackwell, 1992; Southwest Educational Development Laboratory, 2001). However, there must be a varied range of involvement options available to parents that can be tailored to their and their children's individual needs and characteristics. These opportunities should be developmentally appropriate and consistent with the structure, routine, and resources of the school program.

When looking at how you and your school communicate with parents and families, reflect on this: How you choose to communicate with parents sets the tone for the responses you receive.

You may not be able to control whether or not parents give you the support you're looking for, but you certainly can control the manner in which you communicate with them so they feel invited, not intimidated, and appreciated rather than antagonized.

When teachers develop positive relationships with parents, they give their students the best opportunity to get the best possible education. In order to achieve that goal, you must find ways to develop rapport and a team-oriented relationship with families. As we've said, parents sometimes don't make themselves accessible. They may choose not to respond to outreach efforts because they're too busy or simply indifferent. Overcoming a family's lack of interest can be difficult, but certainly not impossible. The more options families have to be involved, the more likely they are to get involved. As Marzano (2003) argues, "it is the responsibility of the school to initiate communication and provide an atmosphere in which parents desire such communication" (p. 48).

There are many factors and areas you can control to establish and improve parental cooperation and set the stage for a mutually beneficial relationship. Here are several communication strategies to consider as you try to involve families in the life of your school:

- **Communicate positive news frequently.** In Chapter 12, we recommended praising students at least four times as often as you correct them. The same ratio works for parents, too. When parents receive a call or note, or are asked to visit school, most cringe because their first thought is that their child is in trouble. Many don't even consider the possibility that a teacher or administrator would take the time to communicate good news. In fact, many parents complain that they only hear about what their children do wrong. Some parents become so discouraged or disgusted by the bad news, they tune out or assume the problem lies with the school, not their child. Emphasizing positive messages, on the other hand, communicates respect and appreciation that can help you connect with parents.

If you do have to make a call about a concern or problem, use the "no fault" approach – emphasize how you and the parents can work together to increase a child's success. Note any attempts the student has made to improve the situation, and end the communication on a positive or hopeful note.

- **Use incentives to get families to regularly come to your school or program.** Activities such as curriculum nights, sharing school lunch with their children, and open classroom policies encourage visits from parents. In secondary schools, something as simple as a pizza dinner (food proves to be a great enticement) or a series of short evening workshops on topics of interest, such as Internet safety, prepping for college, or money matters, can entice parents to make a visit to the school. We know parents do not attend "Back to School" nights or other related functions as frequently when their children move past the elementary grades. To reach parents of older youth, you have to give them a reason to show up. Coming to school to hear an educator talk about policy probably won't interest most of them, but if the event involves their children, more will be motivated to attend.

- **When families do visit, make them feel comfortable.** If language barriers exist, have an interpreter available. Try to understand and respect parents' values and cultures, and praise any positive things or accomplishments their children have done. These efforts will help you establish a relationship with the family, which can improve the child's chances for success.

- **Encourage the use of technology to improve communication.** Sometimes it's difficult for you to reach parents and vice versa because of differing schedules or other logistical issues. So take advantage of communication tools, such as e-mail, webpages, e-newsletters, and phone calls to supplement in-person meetings. These forms of communication can help you stay connected to busy parents. Newsletters that go home regularly or are posted on the Internet are advantageous because they can inform parents about everything from upcoming events to volunteer opportunities to codes of conduct that affect their children. These forms of communication are most effective when they encourage bi-directional dialogue. Whether communicating via print or electronic mediums, include phone numbers, e-mail addresses, hotline numbers, or other appropriate contact information so parents and caregivers know the how, who, and when of contacting the school. As always, be cognizant of your environment and the population you serve. Some – perhaps many – families may not be wired to the web or have access to other electronic tools of communication. Make sure your efforts transcend socioeconomic, geographical, and cultural barriers.

VISIT BOYSTOWN.ORG/PARENTING

When parents are looking for specific suggestions and practical advice about issues affecting their child or teen – academic or behavior problems, bullying, dating, friendships, peer pressure, homework, etc. – send them to boystown.org/parenting. This free online site offers answers and helpful tips to make parenting less stressful and more successful. Teachers tell us they frequently include information from the site in their school newsletters.

- **Use school-home notes when daily communication about skill teaching is necessary.** If a student has ongoing behavioral or academic problems, use a school-home note as a two-way communication device, or "report card," on the student's activities. The note can be an effective way to track and measure the effectiveness of your intervention efforts because it contains up-to-date comments about what's happening in the school and the home. We realize time is an issue, and having a note for every student may be unrealistic. But it is an option when you want to encourage a student's continued practice of a skill outside of school. The note can be as basic as one or two sentences describing the problem and offering the parent advice on how to teach to it.

- **Recruit parent volunteers to help with classroom projects, provide supervision, or be guest lecturers.** Parents have diverse talents and interests that can be used for educational purposes, but the school must first be an inviting environment in order to stimulate interest.

  Tapping into the human capital of your community serves two purposes: You can supplement your staffing needs and build more connections with families in the community. Volunteer opportunities can involve being classroom aides, lunchroom or playground monitors, guest lecturers, tutors, or mentors. Take time to discover the talents of your stakeholders and see if they can be used in creative ways at school.

- **Give parents information about what they can do at home to help students with homework assignments.** Consider developing a regular schedule of homework assignments that require students to interact with parents or other family members. Get families involved in setting student goals each year, including planning for college or work (Epstein et al., 2002). You can also use homework assignments to help students review or reflect on the value of rules, procedures, and consequences. Assignments that involve practicing social skills at home or in the community are a great way to supplement social skills instruction and help students generalize skills beyond the school setting.

- **Include parents in decisions that affect students' school life.** Parents should be involved with the school community on all levels, including district-wide committees. Actively recruit PTA/PTO officers and members. Appoint parents to curriculum, safety, personnel, and other school committees. Develop parent leaders and representatives so your students and school have many passionate advocates (Epstein et al., 2002).

Final Thoughts

Most parents have hopes and goals for their children; they just differ in how they support their children's efforts to achieve those goals. It's important that you initiate relationships, especially with resistant parents. When communicating with parents, assume they know their child and his or her needs better than anyone. Take into consideration their perspective when discussing what you think is best. When you make suggestions, start with something that parents can be successful at implementing. Be willing to compromise when parents disagree. Most importantly, when you communicate, use plain, jargon-free language that everyone can understand.

Educators must have a community-oriented spirit when working with parents, and that spirit must first exist inside the school. The strategies and practices advocated in the previous chapters are practical ways of creating an inclusive, welcoming school climate. If parents are going to be excited and supportive of your efforts, it helps if students have a sense of ownership, excitement, and pride about the school, too. When communication between the school and the home is open, honest, and hopeful, obstacles become less daunting and positive outcomes become more achievable.

Common Sense Parenting

The disruptive and inappropriate behaviors that students demonstrate in your school may have been learned and reinforced in the home. As you look for ways to involve and empower parents in educational activities, some consideration should be given to how prepared and skilled parents are to provide the assistance you seek.

Research shows that when behavior support interventions are implemented in the school (social skills training) and the home (parent training), the positive effects for children are magnified (Pelham & Gnagy, 1999; Harvey, Lewis-Palmer, Horner, & Sugai, 2003).

Boys Town's Common Sense Parenting® complements the philosophy behind our Well-Managed Schools practices. This parent-training program shows parents how to use many of the strategies we've described – Effective Praise, positive and negative consequences, clear expectations, social skills – in their homes. School staff, community volunteers, or students' parents can become Common Sense Parenting trainers and lead workshops for families in your community. To learn more about this opportunity, call 1-800-545-5771 or visit www.boystowntraining.org.

Common Sense Parenting skills are also explained in books and DVDs available through the Boys Town Press at www.boystownpress.org or 1-800-282-6657.

Evaluating Your Well-Managed School

The purpose of classroom and school management is to positively affect student behavior and, ultimately, academic achievement. But simply inserting these strategies into a classroom or school doesn't necessarily guarantee those goals will be met or maintained. All intervention efforts need to be monitored and measured. The information gathered then needs to be acted on to enhance or ensure current and future success.

We realize that schools are already asked to collect and document a vast array of information on students. Fortunately, you do not have to reinvent the wheel when it comes to tracking the progress of your classroom management practices. Much of the information you need may already be at your fingertips or in front of your eyes. Regardless of the specific methods you choose to measure or evaluate behavior changes in a classroom or school, there are two questions that deserve constant consideration:

- Am I using the Well-Managed Schools strategies as they were intended to be used?

- Are these strategies making any difference?

The answers to these questions will tell you whether or not you're moving closer to achieving the healthy, positive social climate you desire and your students deserve. When it comes to the question of "making a difference," here are several information sources that can reveal progress, or lack thereof:

Referral Data – Critical information about behavior problems, people, and places that pose a challenge or who may be at risk can be found in office referral data. From a whole-school perspective, office referral information can be used to prioritize what behavior problems or areas of the school need immediate attention. Discipline referrals also serve as "warning signs of more serious problems likely to occur" (Tobin & Sprague, 2001; p. 155). Answers that can be gleaned from this data include:

- **Where most referrals occur.** Do most originate in the classroom or common areas, such as a cafeteria, restroom, locker room, hallway, and/or parking lot? Using this information, you can increase supervision, establish rules, implement procedures, or use other strategies that target the most problematic environments. If, after implementation, there's a decline in referrals and reported problems, that's a good indicator your interventions are having the desired effect.

- **The behaviors that lead to the referrals.** Are students violating rules or not following procedures? Are they being physically or verbally abusive? Are they taunting, bullying, fighting, or vandalizing school property or others' possessions? Knowing what behaviors are most problematic allows you to better focus your efforts in specific areas, such as putting more emphasis on teaching critical social skills, using more appropriate consequences, or being more proactive in addressing student behavior.

- **The most problematic days or times.** Are most referrals in the morning hours, midday, late afternoon, or during certain transition periods? Is there a spike in referrals on certain days, weeks, or months (after or before extended breaks, prior to significant events, such as a big game or dance, etc.)? In one high school we worked with, office referral data indicated that hallways were relatively calm during morning hours but became more chaotic during and after the lunch periods, when more students arrived late for class. These tardy students were involved in horseplay that often led to verbal and physical fights. Knowing this information, school staff focused on addressing afternoon attendance problems by monitoring transitions from lunch to class more closely and making more announcements about the expectations for student behavior during those times.

- **The students who struggle the most.** Research shows that in elementary and middle schools, less than 10 percent of students account for more than 50 percent of all discipline referrals (Skiba, Peterson, & Williams, 1997; Sprague & Walker, 2000). Some students need more personalized and intensive support than universal intervention strategies provide. Knowing who those students are allows you to develop individualized plans that better support their needs.

- **The staff members who issue the most referrals.** If an individual teacher is responsible for a significant number of office referrals, why is that? It may not be an issue of competence but a matter of circumstance – is the teacher a long-term substitute in the building, have personal life problems, or teach special education students? If a student is frequently referred to the office by the same teacher but has few or no referrals from anyone else, what might be happening in that classroom or with that particular teacher to provoke such a consequence? Is it pure coincidence? A personality conflict? Conflicts with other students in the class? Teacher inexperience? Academic issues? By identifying any patterns or commonalities (the same individuals tend to be involved) that exist, you can develop appropriate solutions (if necessary) that target the real problems.

If you have a reduction in the overall number of referrals, including a decline in how often "frequent flyers" go to the office, after addressing the issues, that's a great indication your efforts are succeeding. If those numbers remain unchanged or worsen, re-evaluate your approach. It's possible additional intervention efforts are required, or more time or consistency is needed in applying your strategies. In some cases, an unanticipated or unexpected event may explain the perceived lack of progress.

In addition to office referrals, behavior incident reports, tardy/truancy reports, and even school nurse data can be used to measure the social climate and safety of your school. For example, recurring visits to the nurse by the same children could indicate a number of potential problems. If a student complains about headaches or stomach pains during a particular class, it may be an excuse to get out of a subject he or she struggles with. Or maybe the child doesn't eat breakfast and is hungry well before lunch. Or, a student could be the target of bullying, intimidation, or harassment in the class, and he or she simply wants to avoid pain and embarrassment. Summarizing data from all these reports can help identify potential problems as well as track your progress in correcting them.

Direct Observations – Observation simply means being attentive to what's happening in the environment. For example, when students walk down the hallway during passing periods:

- Is anyone watching to see who's bumping into others or shouting derogatory comments? (In one school we visited, we counted nine students who hit classmates with a fist during a three-minute passing period. No adults stopped the aggressive students.)

- Does anyone see the couple making out on the stairwell? (This happened during a lunch period when students were supposed to be in class or the cafeteria. Four staff members walked past the students without telling them to stop or get to lunch or class.)

- Does anyone keep an eye on the student who was sent to the hallway because he was disrupting the class? (In one middle school, two males were put in the hallway for talking back and arguing with the teacher. During 10 unsupervised minutes, these two students knocked on other classroom doors, made faces at students in the class, and slid down the hall as if they were stealing second base. Finally, a security guard arrived to take the students to the dean's office.)

Again, from a whole-school perspective, paying attention to student interactions may be the most telling indicator of the general climate of your school. We know that inappropriate actions that go on in common areas like hallways, cafeterias, and locker rooms can carry over into your classrooms and vice versa. By keeping an eye on what goes on throughout the school, you're in a better position to implement strategies that will directly address problems. This proactive stance can keep disruptive and aggressive behavior to a minimum. General observations can be just as valid as more quantitative measures. Hearing less noise and fewer insults in hallways during transitions, seeing more order and cleanliness in the cafeteria during and after lunch, and noticing more cooperation among students in classrooms are visual and auditory signs of progress.

Academic Reports – When problem behaviors decrease and more energy and time is spent on instruction, changes in academic performance can be expected. When looking at student progress in the classroom, academic indicators that your behavior interventions are working include:

- Assignments are completed and turned in on time with greater frequency.

- On-task behavior, especially during in-class projects and group work, increases.

- Scores on unit tests, chapter quizzes, and standardized tests improve.

- Attendance improves while tardiness, suspensions, and detentions decline.

Informal Conversations with Stakeholders – Informal conversations among all stakeholders is an underused, and sometimes undervalued, source of information. Besides being exercises in relationship building, these casual chats also can reveal important opinions about what works and why, and what problems may be lurking just beneath the surface:

- **Chats with colleagues.** Collegial relationships among staff are as vital to the health of a school's social climate as any other relationship between stakeholders. If you're struggling with a student or situation, seek advice from peers. Likewise, if a colleague comes to you with a concern, be willing to listen. If you're an administrator, seek regular feedback from all staff, including teachers, bus drivers, cafeteria workers, and administrative support personnel. Ask them if they're concerned about any students or if they feel something could be done better to make areas of the school less chaotic. Be open and receptive to their comments and suggestions. The sign of a well-functioning school is that everyone takes ownership in its success. Acknowledging others' ideas and opinions reinforces efforts to create an inclusive, team-oriented culture.

- **Chats with parents.** In the previous chapter, we discussed ways to increase your positive contacts with parents. There are many opportunities to have informal conversations with them, such as parent-teacher meetings, when they're dropping off or picking up students, or during a phone call to report on a student's success. If you make just one or two calls or contacts a day, at the end of two weeks, you will have reached as many as a dozen parents. Remember, increasing positive interactions with parents can result in more support from them. They also may be more willing to discuss sensitive issues or share concerns in ways that attack a problem rather than the school, its staff, or you.

- **Chats with students.** Don't be afraid or hesitant to ask students how they feel about what's going on in your classroom or school. Questions such as, "How are things on the playground?" or "Have you noticed anyone having problems in the locker rooms?" might reveal the presence or absence of problems, including harassment and bullying. Students can even provide input on how to make things work more smoothly in a classroom, or tell you what they like or dislike about certain rules and procedures.

An individual conversation with a staff member, parent, or student may not always provide a complete or accurate picture of the social climate. But when all the stakeholders are given opportunities to share their thoughts – through many different forums – the success of your intervention strategies and their effect on the overall social climate can reveal itself.

Personal Measures of Satisfaction – Are there signs your personal outlook and health are improving? While consulting with school staff members in a very challenging environment, we asked how their implementation of the Well-Managed Schools program was going. One teacher replied, "I no longer get sick in the morning before I come to school." The stress of dealing with aggressive students and all the negativity inside the school had adversely affected his health. Another teacher said, "I used to be worn out and tired at the end of the day. Now I realize it's my job to help my students feel worn out and tired." Both teachers had been feeling emotionally drained and beaten up at the end of their workday. They were physically wiped out by all the chaos and hostility. But after implementing several behavior-management strategies into their school day, they were able to keep their students challenged, busy, and on task. Now, it was their students who were getting worn out because of all the learning that was occurring in their classrooms.

Improvements in your physical and mental health, reflected in better attendance at work and a more hopeful outlook about your job and profession, are a personal way of measuring success.

A Self-Assessment

There may be times when progress slows and behavior problems persist. Don't let such moments discourage you. Instead, reflect on how well you are implementing and using the practices and strategies of a well-managed school.

It takes time and energy to create and maintain a cooperative, productive, and collaborative learning environment. Yet that's only one of many responsibilities and goals you are working toward. There are many professional obligations and duties you are expected to fulfill. So, it's to be expected and certainly understandable if the big picture sometimes gets lost and certain strategies go by the wayside. For example, we had a teacher tell us that classroom rules were useless. Students ignored her rules year after year, and behavior problems only seemed to get worse. A visit to her classroom revealed that she did have rules posted, but they were in the back of the room, partially obscured. The rules had hung in the same spot the past four years with no changes. And while she went over the rules with her students at the start of the year, she never reviewed them later or taught students the skills they needed to follow them. Students were rarely reinforced for following the rules, and the rules didn't always reflect the abilities or problems of the students. No consideration was given to the fact that each new academic year brought a completely different group of children together who had their own social dynamics. Her attempt to shape behavior in the classroom was undermined by actions and attitudes that could only be described as inconsistent and indifferent.

What would have helped this teacher – and what we recommend you do – is to reflect on your goals every day, not once a quarter or semester, or at the end of an academic year. Ask yourself:

- Am I connecting with my students? Do I make an effort to greet them in the halls or when they enter my class? Am I listening to them and showing enthusiasm for their goals and interests?

- Do I empower them to make better choices? Have I taught students the SODAS or POP decision-making process so they are better able to solve problems and resolve conflicts? When students make good decisions, do I acknowledge their choices?

- Do I explain behavior expectations to students? When they make a behavioral mistake, am I using objective, specific language to describe the problem so there is little misunderstanding or debate?

- Do I use rationales that motivate my students? Are they meaningful and believable? Can students understand the benefits of learning social skills or following rules and procedures?

- Do I have rules posted in my classroom and around the school? Are procedures in place to deal with problematic transitions or chaotic periods of the day? Am I reviewing the rules and procedures periodically with students?

- Do I actively teach social skills to students? Are there skills that need to be re-taught or emphasized?

- Do I praise my students enough? Am I using the 4:1 positive-to-negative ratio? Am I looking for the positive things students do or do their inappropriate actions consume my attention?

- Do I model the behaviors I expect to see from my students? Am I setting a good example for students to follow, especially when I'm correcting behavior or working with an emotionally intense youth? Am I using empathy statements and other corrective strategies to calm students and prevent their behaviors from escalating?

- Do I use consequences that are meaningful to the students rather than to me? Are the consequences changing negative behaviors and reinforcing positive ones? Do I use role-plays and practice to show students alternative ways of handling situations and problems?

- Am I using Planned Teaching, blended teaching, preventive prompts, and other methods to teach skills and reinforce behavior expectations?

- Am I using the Well-Managed Schools practices as they were intended to be used?

Final Thoughts

On the following pages, we've included a sample Teacher Survey you can complete or refer to at any time. This self-assessment exercise encourages you to review and reflect on how well you are using the classroom management strategies described throughout this manual.

We hope you've learned methods, techniques, and skills that enhance your professional repertoire. Like you, we want all students to experience success in school, be it academic, vocational, athletic, or artistic. Yet it's critically important that success not be defined solely in terms of passing grades and acceptable test scores. Young people also have emotional, behavioral, and social needs. Therefore, the learning environments we create for our children must give them the structure, support, sense of connectedness, and safety that allows them to develop their individual talents and realize their full potential.

Teacher Survey

This survey provides information about how teachers use classroom management strategies. Please darken the circle that most closely matches your response on each item or write your response where indicated.

		NEVER	SOMETIMES	OFTEN	ALWAYS
1	I provided planned instruction in social skills.	O	O	O	O
2	I provided spontaneous teaching of social skills.	O	O	O	O
3	I used class activities, student behavior, and/or discipline referral trends to direct the planned instruction of social skills in the classroom.	O	O	O	O
4	I praised students for their social behavior.	O	O	O	O
5	I praised students for their academic performance.	O	O	O	O
6	I praised students more often than I corrected them for their social behavior.	O	O	O	O
7	When I corrected student misbehavior, I explained to them what they should do instead of the misbehavior.	O	O	O	O
8	Students in my class(es) were on task during academic lessons.	O	O	O	O
9	Students in my class(es) transitioned to other classes and activities in an orderly fashion.	O	O	O	O
10	Students in my class(es) talked nicely to each other.	O	O	O	O
11	Students in my class(es) entered class prepared to work.	O	O	O	O
12	Students in my class(es) argued with each other.	O	O	O	O

13 Students in my class(es) fought
with each other.   O   O   O   O

14 Students in my class(es)
followed my directions.   O   O   O   O

15 Students in my class(es) stopped
their misbehavior right away when
I corrected them.   O   O   O   O

16 In general, I used the strategies
from Well-Managed Schools.   O   O   O   O

17 My principal encouraged teachers
to use Well-Managed Schools
practices.   O   O   O   O

18 During daily school announcements,
my principal mentioned the name
of a social skill.   O   O   O   O

19 During daily school announcements,
my principal talked about how to
use a social skill.   O   O   O   O

	YES	NO
20 I have rules for student behavior clearly posted in my classroom.	O	O
21 We have rules for student behavior posted in common areas throughout the school.	O	O
22 My school emphasizes a social skill of the week or month throughout the school year.	O	O

If "Yes," please write the social skill for this past week or month here:

_____

23 What individual or process was most influential in my decision
to implement Well-Managed Schools strategies? _____

_____

About the Authors

Michele Hensley, M.S., has 17 years of teaching experience at the high school and middle school levels in San Antonio, Texas, and Omaha, Nebraska. For nine years, she worked with teachers and school administrators as a consultant and trainer for Boys Town. Hensley is a co-author of *Tools for Teaching Social Skills in School,* and is a science instructor at Boys Town High School.

Walter Powell previously was the Assistant Director of Education Services for Boys Town. He has been instrumental in the direction, development, and delivery of training and consultation services based on the Boys Town Education Model®. For the past 10 years, Powell has provided staff development training to teachers, support staff, and administrators, as well as conducted on-site school-wide assessments and consultation services in more than 100 school districts throughout the United States. He also has authored numerous articles for professional journals.

Susan Lamke, M.S., is Manager of Boys Town's Learning Technology and Curricula. She provides consultation services and support to school systems across the country that implement the Boys Town Education Model. She has conducted hundreds of workshops, including Well-Managed Schools and Specialized Classroom Management, for teachers, paraprofessionals, administrators, and guidance counselors. Lamke has also taught at the elementary level for Omaha Public Schools.

Scott A. Hartman, M.S., previously was director of the Education Training Division at Boys Town. An educator with more than 20 years of experience working with and on behalf of youth, he has a master's degree in human service administration. He taught school in Indiana before becoming a Family-Teacher in Boys Town's Family Home Program℠. Hartman has held a variety of positions in direct care, training, and administration at Boys Town. He is also president of his local Home and School Association.

Michael Meeks, M.S., is the Manager of National Training at Boys Town. He has worked at Boys Town for 16 years as a behavioral interventionist, trainer, and consultant, advising hundreds of schools and organizations across the country on effective systems for managing student behavior.

Erin Green, M.S., is the Director of National Training and Boys Town Press Services for Boys Town's Youth Care Division. As a parent and educator, Green has worked with youth of all ages, including those with special needs, mental health diagnoses, and emotional/behavioral disorders. She also speaks at conferences and is a national trainer and author. Green currently oversees the Boys Town Press® as well as the design and development of Boys Town Model® training and consultation services and their delivery to schools and agencies, nationally and internationally.

References

Alberto, P.A., & Troutman, A.C. (2006). **Applied behavior analysis for teachers,** (7th ed.). Upper Saddle River, NJ: Pearson Prentice Hall.

Astor, R.A., Benbenishty, R., & Meyer, H.A. (2004). Monitoring and mapping student victimization in schools. **Theory into Practice, 43**(1), 39-49.

Baddeley, A.D. (1986) **Working memory.** Oxford: Clarendon Press.

Baker, J.A., Terry, T., Bridger, R., & Winsor, A. (1997). Schools as caring communities: A relational approach to school reform. **School Psychology Review, 26**(4), 586-602.

Bandura, A. (1979). Self-referent mechanisms in social learning theory. **American Psychologist, 34**(5), 439-441. doi:10.1037/0003-066X.34.5.439.b

Bandura, A. (1986). **Social foundations of thought and action: A social cognitive theory.** Englewood Cliffs, NJ: Prentice-Hall.

Barkley, R.A. (2012). **Executive functions: What they are, how they work, and why they evolved.** New York: Guilford Press.

Bluestein, J. (2001). **21st century discipline: Teaching students responsibility and self-control,** (2nd ed.). Grand Rapids, MI: Frank Schaffer.

Blum, R.W. (2005). A case for school connectedness. **Educational Leadership, 62**(7), 16-20.

Bullis, M., Walker, H.M., & Stieber, S. (1998). The influence of peer and educational variables on arrest status among at-risk males. **Journal of Emotional and Behavioral Disorders, 6**(3), 141-152.

Burch, P., & Palanki, A. (1994). Parent-teacher action research: Supporting families through family-school-community partnerships. **Journal of Emotional and Behavioral Problems, 2**(4), 16-18.

Burke, R., O'Neill Fichtner, L., Oats, R., Johnson, S., DelGaudio, M., & Powell, W. (2007). Relationships among model fidelity, dosage, and student outcomes in high risk elementary schools. In C. Newman, C.J. Liberton, K. Kutash, and R.M. Friedman (Eds.), **The 19th annual research conference proceedings: A system of care for children's mental health: Expanding the research base** (pp. 215-218). Tampa: University of South Florida, Louis de la Parte Florida Mental Health Institute, Research and Training Center for Children's Mental Health.

Burke, R.V., Guck, T.P., Robinson, M.L., Powell, W., & O'Neill Fichtner, L. (2006). Overcoming resistance to implementing classroom management strategies: Use of the transtheoretical model to explain teacher behavior. **Research in the Schools, 13**(2), 1-12.

Carr, E.G., Dunlap, G., Horner, R.H., Koegel, R.L., Turnbull, A.P., Sailor, W., Anderson, J.L., Albin, R.W., Koegel, L.K., & Fox, L. (2002). Positive behavior support: Evolution of an applied science. **Journal of Positive Behavior Interventions, 4**(1), 4-16, 20.

Cartledge, G., & Milburn, J.F. (1978). The case for teaching social skills in the classroom: A review. **Review of Educational Research, 48**(1), 133-156.

Catalano, R.F., Haggerty, K.P., Oesterle, S., Fleming, C.B., & Hawkins, J.D. (2004). The importance of bonding to school for healthy development: Findings from the social development research group. **Journal of School Health, 74**(7), 252-261.

Catsambis, S., & Garland, J.E. (1997). **Parental involvement in students' education during middle and high school (Report 18)**. Baltimore, MD: John Hopkins University, Center for Research on the Education of Students Placed at Risk.

Center on the Developing Child at Harvard University (2011). **Building the brain's "air traffic control" system: How early experiences shape the development of executive function: Working paper no. 11.** Retrieved from http://www.developing child.harvard.edu

Coie, J.D., & Jacobs, M.R. (1993). The role of social context in the pre-vention of conduct disorder. **Development and Psychopathology, 5,** 263-275.

Collaborative for Academic, Social, and Emotional Learning. (2012). **2013 CASEL guide: Effective social and emotional learning programs–Preschool and elementary school edition.** Chicago, IL: Author.

Collaborative for Academic, Social, and Emotional Learning. (2013). **CASEL school kit: A guide to implementing school-wide academic, social, and emotional learning.** Chicago: Author.

Colvin, G., Kame'enui, E.J., & Sugai, G. (1993). Reconceptualizing behavior management and school-wide discipline in general ed-ucation. **Education and Treatment of Children, 16**(4), 361-381.

Commission on Children At Risk. (2003). **Hardwired to connect: The new scientific case for authoritative communities.** New York: Institute for American Values.

Cooper, J.O., Heron, T.E., & Heward, W.L. (1987). **Applied behavior analysis.** Columbus, OH: Prentice Hall.

Cooper, J.O., Heron, T.E., & Heward, W.L. (2006). **Applied behavior analysis,** (2nd ed.). Columbus, OH: Prentice Hall.

Crosnoe, R. (2001). Academic orientation and parental involvement in education during high school. **Sociology of Education, 74**(3), 210-230.

DePaul, A. (1998). **What to expect your first year of teaching.** Washington, DC: United States Department of Education, Office of Educational Research and Improvement.

Domina, T. (2005). Leveling the home advantage: Assessing the effec-tiveness of parental involvement in elementary school. **Sociology of Education, 78**(3), 233-249.

Downs, J., Black, D., & Kutsick, K. (1985). The teaching interaction: A systematic approach to developing social skills in disruptive and non-disruptive students. **Techniques: A Journal for Remedial Education and Counseling, 1**(4), 304-310.

Epstein, J.L., Sanders, M.G., Simon, B.S., Salinas K.C., Jansorn, N.R., & Van Voorhis, F.L. (2002). **School, family, and community partnerships: Your handbook for action,** (2nd ed.). Thousand Oaks, CA: Corwin Press.

Eitzen, D.S. (1974). Impact of behavior modification techniques on locus of control of delinquent boys. **Psychological Reports, 35**(3), 1,317-1,318.

Elias, M.J., Parker, S.J., Kash, V.M., Weissberg, R.P., & O'Brien, M.U. (2008). Social and emotional learning, moral education, and character education: A comparative analysis and a view toward convergence. **Handbook of Moral and Character Education,** 248-266.

Evertson, C.M., & Emmer, E.T. (1982). Effective management at the beginning of the school year in junior high classes. **Journal of Educational Psychology, 74**(4), 485-498.

Fredrickson, B.L., & Losada, M.F. (2005). Positive affect and the complex dynamics of human flourishing. **American Psychologist, 60**(7), 678-686.

Glasser, W. (1998). **Choice theory in the classroom.** New York: HarperCollins.

Goldstein, A.P. (1999). **The prepare curriculum: Teaching prosocial competencies.** Champaign, IL: Research Press.

Goleman, D. (2005). **Emotional intelligence: 10th anniversary edition; Why it can matter more than IQ.** New York: Bantam Dell.

Gottman, J.M. (1998). **Why marriages succeed or fail and how you can make yours last.** London: Bloomsbury Publishing Plc.

Harvey, M.T., Lewis-Palmer, T., Horner R.H., & Sugai, G. (2003). Trans-situational interventions: Generalization of behavior support across school and home environments. **Behavioral Disorders, 28**(3), 299-312.

Henderlong, J., & Lepper, M.R. (2002). The effects of praise on children's intrinsic motivation: A review and synthesis. **Psychological Bulletin, 128**(5), 774-795.

Hernandez, T.J., & Seem, S.R. (2004). A safe school climate: A systematic approach and the school counselor. **Professional School Counseling, 7**(4), 256-262.

Horner, R.H., Sugai, G., Lewis-Palmer, T., & Todd, A.W. (2001). Teaching school-wide behavioral expectations. **Report on Emotional and Behavioral Disorders in Youth, 1**(4), 77-96.

Horner, R.H., Sugai, G., & Anderson, C.M. (2010). Examining the evidence base for school-wide positive behavior support. **Focus on Exceptional Children, 42**(8), 1-14. Retrieved from http://ezproxy.bellevue.edu:80/login?url – http://search.proquest.com.ezproxy.bellevue.edu/docview/808393227?accountid = 28125

Hughes, J.N., Cavell, T.A., & Willson, V. (2001). Further support for the developmental significance of the quality of the teacher-student relationship. **Journal of School Psychology, 39**(4), 289-301.

Jiang, J., Econo, M., & Skinner, C. (2016). **National Center for Childhood Poverty: Basic facts about low income children.** Retrieved from http://www.nccp.org/publications/pub_1145.html

Jones, V., & Jones, L. (2007). **Comprehensive classroom management: Creating communities of support and solving problems,** (8th ed.). Boston: Pearson Education.

Juster, F.T., Ono, H., & Stafford, F.P. (2004). **Changing times of American youth: 1981-2003.** Ann Arbor: University of Michigan, Institute for Social Research.

Kann, L., Kinchen, S., Shanklin, S.L., Flint, K.H., Kawkins, J., Harris, W.A., & Whittle, L. (2014). Youth risk behavior surveillance – United States, 2013. **MMWR Surveillance Summary, 63**(Suppl 4), 1-168.

Kaplan, J.S., & Drainville B. (1990). **Beyond behavior modification: A cognitive-behavioral approach to behavior management in the school,** (2nd ed.). Austin, TX: Pro-Ed.Klem, A.M., & Connell, J.P. (2004). Relationships matter: Linking teacher support to student engagement and achievement. **Journal of School Health, 74**(7), 262-273.

Kohn, A. (2004). Safety from the inside out: Rethinking traditional approaches. **Educational Horizons, 83**(1), 33-41.

Lewis, C.C., Schaps, E., & Watson, M.S. (1996). The caring class-room's academic edge. **Educational Leadership, 51**(1), 16-21.

Lewis, T. (1997). **Responsible decision making about effective behavioral support.** (ERIC Document Reproduction Service No. ED413692).

Libbey, H.P. (2004). Measuring student relationships to school: Attachment, bonding, connectedness, and engagement. **Journal of School Health, 74**(7), 274-283.

Long, N.J., (1995). Why adults strike back: Learned behavior or genetic code? **Reclaiming Children and Youth, 4**(1), 11-15.

Long, N.J., & Wood, M.M. (1990). **Life space intervention: Talking with children and youth in crisis.** Austin, TX: Pro-Ed.

Long, N.J., Wood, M.M., & Fecser, F.A. (2001). **Life space crisis intervention: Talking with students in conflict.** Austin, TX: Pro-Ed.

Mannan, G., & Blackwell, J. (1992). Parent involvement: Barriers and opportunities. **The Urban Review, 24**(3), 219-226.

Marzano, R.J. (2003). **What works in schools: Translating research into action.** Alexandria, VA: Association for Supervision and Curriculum Development.

Mayer, G.R. (1999). Constructive discipline for school personnel. **Education and Treatment of Children, 22**(1), 36-54.

McNeal Jr., R.B. (1999). Parental involvement as social capital: Differential effectiveness on science achievement, truancy, and dropping out. **Social Forces, 78**(1), 117-144.

McNeely, C., & Falci, C. (2004). School connectedness and the transition into and out of health-risk behavior among adolescents: A comparison of social belonging and teacher support. **Journal of School Health, 74**(7), 284-292.

McNeely, C.A., Nonnemaker, J.M., & Blum, R.W. (2002). Promoting school connectedness: Evidence from the national longitudinal study of adolescent health. **Journal of School Health, 72**(4), 138-146.

Meadows, N., Neel, R.S., Parker, G., & Timo, K. (1991). A validation of social skills for students with behavioral disorders. **Behavioral Disorders, 16**(3), 200-210.

MetLife Survey of The American Teacher (2004-2005). **Transitions and the role ofsupportive relationships** [Online]. Available: http://www.metlife.com/WPSAssets/34996838801118758796V1F ATS_2004.pdf.

MetLife Survey of The American Teacher (2008). **The American teacher: Past, present, and future.** Retrieved from www.files. eric.ed.gov/fulltext/504457.pdf

Miller, C.S. (1984). Building self-control: Discipline for young children. **Young Children, 40**(1), 15-19.

Morin, A. (2014, March). **Understanding executive function issues.** Retrieved from https://www.understood.org/en/learning-atten- tion-issues/child-learning-disabilities/executive-functioning-is- sues/understanding-executive-functioning-issues

National Center for Children in Poverty (2006). **Who are America's poor children?** The official story [Online]. Available: http:// www.nccp.org/pub_cpt06a.html.

National Commission on Teaching and America's Future (2003). **No dream denied: A pledge to America's children.** Washington, DC: Author.

National Institute of Mental Health. **Attention-Deficit Hyperactivity Disorder.** Bethesda (MD): National Institute of Mental Health, National Institutes of Health, U.S. Department of Health and Hu- man Services; 2006 [cited 2007 May 11]. (NIH Publication Num- ber: 3572). 49 pages. Available from: http://www.nimh.nih.gov/ publicat/NIMHadhdpub.pdf.

National Institute of Mental Health (2007). **Child and adolescent mental health** [Online]. Available: http://www.nimh.nih.gov/ healthinformation/childmenu.cfm.

Noguera, P.A. (1995). Preventing and producing violence: A critical analysis of response to school violence. **Harvard Educational Review, 65**(2), 189-212.

Noonan, J. (2004). School climate and the safe school: Seven contributing factors. **Educational Horizons, 83**(1), 61-65.

Oats, R., Faulk, A. Gulley, T.J., Hensley, M.M., & Burke, R.V. (2006, February). **Reducing aggressive and disruptive behavior with a school-wide classroom management program: Replication of effects at two sites.** Paper presented at the Midwest Symposium on Leadership in Behavior Disorders, Kansas City, MO.

Olafson, L., & Field, J.C. (2003). A moral revisioning of resistance. **Educational Forum, 67**(2), 140-147.

Olweus, D. (1991). Bully/victim problems among schoolchildren: Basic facts and effects of a school-based intervention program. In D.J. Pepler & K.H. Rubin (Eds.), **The development and treatment of childhood aggression** (pp. 441-448). Mahwah, NJ: Lawrence Erlbaum Assoc.

Pelham, W.E., & Gnagy, E.M. (1999). Psychosocial and combined treatments for ADHD. **Mental Retardation and Developmental Disabilities Research Reviews, 5,** 225-236.

Porter, A., & Brophy, J. (1988). Synthesis of research on good teaching: Insights from the work of the institute for research on teaching. **Educational Leadership, 45**(8), 74-85.

Prawat, R.S., & Nickerson, J.R. (1985). The relationship between teacher thought and action and student affective outcomes. **The Elementary School Journal, 85**(4), 529-540.

Pribram, K.H. (1973). The primate frontal cortex-executive of the brain. **Psychophysiology of the Frontal Lobes,** 293-314.

Pribram, K.H. (1976). Executive functions of the frontal lobe. In T. Desiraju (Ed.), **The transmission of signals for conscious behavior** (pp. 303-300). Amsterdam: Elsevier Science & Technology.

Public Agenda (2004). **Teaching interrupted: Do discipline policies in today's public schools foster the common good?** [Online]. Available: http://www.publicagenda.org/research/pdfs/teaching_interrupted_exec_summary.pdf.

Public Agenda (2006). **Reality check 2006: How black and Hispanic families rate their schools** [Online]. Available: http://www.publicagenda.org/research/pdfs/rc0602.pdf.

Resnick, M.D., Harris, L.J., & Blum, R.W. (1993). The impact of caring and connectedness on adolescent health and well-being. **Journal of Paediatrics and Child Health, 29,** 3-9.

Roosa, J.B. (1973). **SOCS: Situations, options, consequences, simulations: A technique for teaching social interactions.** Paper presented at the American Psychological Association, Montreal, Canada.

Search Institute (2007). **The 40 developmental assets for adolescents** [Online]. Available: http://www.search-institute.org/assets.

Simonsen, B., Sugai, G., & Negron, M. (2008). School-wide positive behavior supports: Primary systems and practices. **Teaching Exceptional Children, 40**(6), 32-40. Retrieved from http://ezproxy.bellevue.edu:80/login?url = http://search.proquest.com.ezproxy.bellevue.edu/docview/201186544?accountid = 28125

Skiba, R.J., & Peterson, R.L. (2000). School discipline at a crossroads: From zero tolerance to early response. **Exceptional Children, 66**(3), 335-346.

Skiba, R.J., Peterson, R.L., & Williams, T. (1997). Office referrals and suspensions: Disciplinary intervention in middle schools. **Education and Treatment of Children, 20**(3), 295-315.

Solomon, D., Watson, M.S., Delucchi, K.L., Schaps, E., & Battistich, V. (1988). Enhancing children's prosocial behavior in the classroom. **American Educational Research Journal, 25**(4), 527-554.

Southwest Educational Development Laboratory (2001). **Emerging key issues in school, family, and community connections.** Austin, TX: Author.

Spivack, G., & Schure, M.B. (1974). **Social adjustment of young children: A cognitive approach to solving real-life problems.** San Francisco: Jossey-Bass.

Sprague, J., & Walker, H. (2000). Early identification and intervention for youth with antisocial and violent behavior. **Exceptional Children, 66**(3), 367-379.

Steinberg, Z., & Knitzer, J. (1992). Classrooms for emotionally and behaviorally disturbed students: Facing the challenge. **Behavioral Disorders, 17**(2), 145-156.

Strauch, B. (2003). **The primal teen: What the new discoveries about the teenage brain tell us about our kids.** New York: Doubleday.

Sugai, G., & Horner, R.H. (2006). A promising approach for expanding and sustaining school-wide positive behavior support. **School Psychology Review, 35**(2), 245.

Sugai, G., & Horner, R.H. (2009). Responsiveness-to-intervention and school-wide positive behavior supports: Integration of multi-tiered system approaches. **Exceptionality, 17**(4), 223-237.

Sugai, G., Horner, R.H., & Gresham, F.M. (2002). Behaviorally effective school environments. In M.R. Shinn, H.M. Walker, and G. Stoner (Eds.), **Interventions for academic and behavior problems II: Preventive and remedial approaches** (pp. 315-350). Bethesda, MD: National Association of School Psychologists.

Sugai, G., Sprague, J.R., Horner, R.H., & Walker, H.M. (2000). Preventing school violence: The use of office discipline referrals to assess and monitor school-wide discipline interventions. **Journal of Emotional and Behavioral Disorders, 8**(2), 94-101.

Taylor, A.R. (1989). Predictors of peer rejection in early elementary grades: Roles of problem behavior, academic achievement, and teacher preference. **Journal of Clinical Child Psychology, 18**(4), 360-365.

Taylor-Greene, S., Brown, D., Nelson, L., Longton, J., Gassman, T., Cohen, J., Swartz, J., Horner, R. H., Sugai, G., & Hall, S. (1997). School-wide behavioral support: Starting the year off right. **Journal of Behavioral Education, 7**(1), 99-112.

Tierney, J., Green, E., & Dowd, T. (2016). **Teaching social skills to youth: An easy-to-follow guide to teaching 183 basic to complex life skills** (3rd ed.). Boys Town, NE: Boys Town Press.

Tobin, T., & Sprague, J. (2001). Alternative education strategies: Reducing violence in school and the community. In H.M. Walker & M.H. Epstein (Eds.), **Making schools safer and violence free: Critical issues, solutions, and recommended practices** (pp. 150-159). Austin, TX: Pro-Ed.

Walker, H.M. (1998). First steps to prevent antisocial behavior. **Teaching Exceptional Children, 30**(4), 16-19.

Walker, H.M., Ramsey, E., & Gresham, F.M. (Eds.). (2004). **Antisocial behavior in school: Evidence-based practices,** (2nd ed.). Belmont, CA: Wadsworth/Thomson Learning.

Walker, H.M., & Sprague, J.R. (1999). The path to school failure, delinquency, and violence: Causal factors and some potential solutions. **Intervention in School and Clinic, 35**(2), 67-73.

Willert, H.J., & Lenhardt, A.M.C. (2003). Tackling school violence does take the whole village. **Educational Forum, 67**(2), 110-118.

Wilson, B.A., Evans, J.J., Alderman, N., Burgess, P.W., & Emslie, H. (1997). Behavioural assessment of the dysexecutive syndrome. **Methodology of Frontal and Executive Function,** 239-250.

White, O.R., & Haring, N.G. (1980). **Exceptional Teaching,** (2nd ed.). Columbus, OH: Merrill Publishing Company.

Wong, H.K., & Wong, R.T. (2004). **The first days of school: How to be an effective teacher.** Mountain View, CA: Harry K. Wong Publications.

Woolfolk Hoy, A., & Weinstein, C.S. (2006). Students' and teachers' perspectives on classroom management. In C.M. Evertson & C.S. Weinstein (Eds.), **Handbook for classroom management: Research, practice and contemporary issues** (pp. 181-220). Mahwah, NJ: Lawrence Erlbaum Assoc.

Wynn, J., Meyer, S., & Richards-Schuster, K. (2000). Furthering education: The relationship of schools and other organizations. In M.C.

Wang & W.L. Boyd (Eds.), **Improving results for children and families: Linking collaborative services with school reform efforts** (pp. 53-90). Greenwich, CT: Information Age Publishing.

Index

S